BUILDING WEALTH — THROUGH — RENTAL PROPERTIES

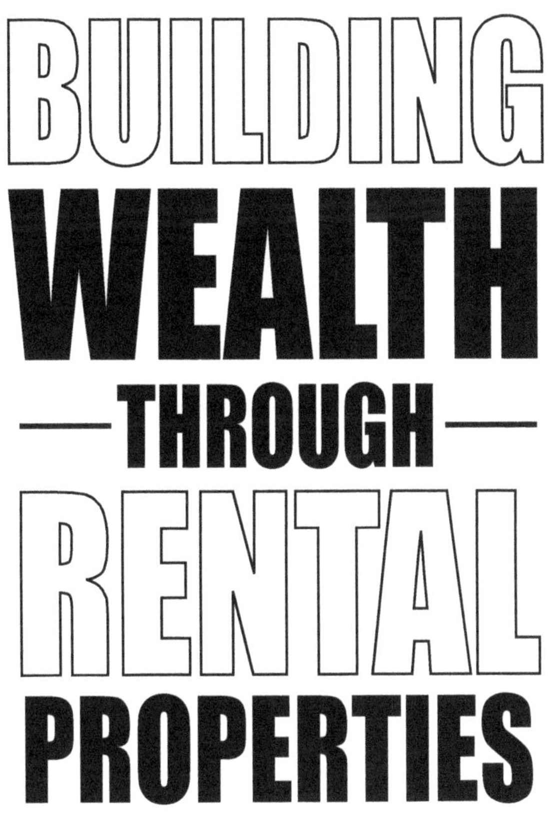

BUILDING WEALTH THROUGH RENTAL PROPERTIES

DR. AMIT SACHDEO

Library of Congress Control Number: 2024941695

ISBN (hardcover): 9781662953521
ISBN (paperback): 9781662953514
eISBN: 9781662953538

DEDICATION

To my two lifelines and superheroes—my parents,
Kiran Sachdeo and **Jogesh Sachdeo.**
Their unconditional love, steadfast support, endless sacrifices,
and profound blessings have illuminated my path through life and molded me
into the person I am today. Thank you for being my constant source
of motivation and strength.

And

To the Almighty for everything!

TABLE OF CONTENTS

Acknowledgments 1

Introduction 3

Preface 5

Chapter 1 What Is a Rental Investment Property? 11

Chapter 2 Types of Rental Properties 23

Chapter 3 Partnerships in Rental Investment Properties 31

Chapter 4 Tax Incentives for Rental Properties 43

Chapter 5 The CAP Tripod™ 51

Chapter 6 Incorporating a Rental Property 129

Chapter 7 The Seven R's™ 139

Chapter 8 The Good, the Bad, the Ugly 163

Chapter 9 Checklist 169

Chapter 10 Resources 175

Chapter 11 Comprehensive Glossary 181

ACKNOWLEDGMENTS

My sincerest gratitude and appreciation to the following:

Late Sri. Jagatri Lal Sachdeo, Late Smt. Harbans Kumari Sachdeo, Late Sardar Chanan Singh Bhasin, and **Late Smt. Raj Rani Bhasin,** my beloved grandparents and guardian angels. Forever in my heart, their wisdom, affection, and blessings inspire me each and every day.

Barry J. Bisson, my best friend, partner, and pillar of strength, whose unwavering love and support have been the cornerstone of my journey, empowering me to pursue my dreams and confidently overcome challenges.

Sumit Sachdeo, my darling older brother; **Priyanka Sachdeo**, my beautiful sister-in-law; and **Nitin Sachdeo**, my adorable nephew, for their encouragement, understanding, and belief in me. Together, we have enjoyed laughter, weathered storms, and created lasting memories that I hold extremely close to my heart.

Gaurav Sachdeo, my caring little brother and eternal cheerleader. I am incredibly grateful for having you in my life and for all the moments we have shared.

My family and friends, for always being by my side and brightening my life with warmth, laughter, and a sense of belonging that I cherish deeply.

INTRODUCTION

"Real estate is an imperishable asset, ever increasing in value.
It is the most solid security that human ingenuity has devised.
It is the basis of all security and about the only
indestructible security."

—RUSSELL SAGE, American financier and politician

In the ever-evolving landscape of investment opportunities, real estate stands out as a powerful wealth-building tool that has stood the test of time. If you are completely new to rental property investing, *Building Wealth through Rental Properties* serves as a comprehensive roadmap to mastering the exciting world of real estate investing.

Packed with practical advice and actionable strategies, this handbook covers everything novice investors need to build a successful rental property portfolio from the ground up. Each chapter is crafted to empower readers with the knowledge, strategies, and confidence needed to unlock the wealth-building potential of real estate. Inside, readers will find the motivation to transform aspirations of wealth and prosperity into an abundant reality of financial freedom.

The language and layout of this book are simple and straightforward, making the process of rental property investing easy to understand for individuals from all walks of life.

Start-to-finish key steps include:

- Strategies for making wealth through rental properties.
- How to identify lucrative rental properties.
- Optimal financing methods for investing in rental properties.
- The entire process from the onset to the final purchase of a rental property.
- Tips for effective property management.
- Proven methods for expanding a rental property portfolio.
- Real-life case studies to inform, inspire, and bolster confidence.
- A comprehensive glossary of essential terms with understandable definitions.
- And so much more—all tailored for maximum relevance and understanding!

PREFACE

"If you don't own a home, buy one. If you own a home, buy another one. If you own two homes, buy a third."

—JOHN PAULSON, American billionaire hedge fund manager

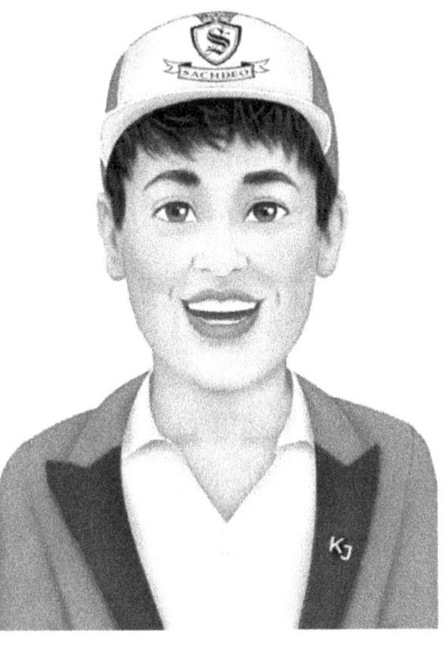

My journey in the world of real estate began soon after I graduated from Harvard University and started my first job in Boston. Although I had a significant amount of student loan debt upon graduation, I was able to secure a bank loan to purchase a small one-bedroom condominium in the city. That summer, when my parents visited me, the one-bedroom condominium seemed relatively small for all of us. My mother suggested I purchase another condominium in the same building if the opportunity ever arose. This would give my parents their own space when they visit in the future and supplement my income by renting out the condominium once they leave.

I took my mother's advice and used additional savings to purchase a second condominium in the same building. Before long, I noticed that after covering the bank loan and other costs associated with the second condominium, there was still a modest surplus of rental income each month. What was initially intended as a comfortable space for my parents during their visits, the second condominium soon evolved into a strategic investment endeavor. Little did I realize that this also marked the inception of my real estate journey.

Soon after, I started investing in additional rental properties as a viable strategy for creating a steady stream of passive income. With significant guidance from my father, an engineer by profession, I examined the potential returns of various properties and began expanding my real estate holdings. I started with a one-bedroom condominium but then quickly moved on to single-family homes, then two-family homes, and eventually multi-family apartment buildings. I further diversified my portfolio by investing in parking garages and commercial triple-net properties. With unwavering determination and belief in the transformative power of real estate, I embarked on a path of strategic investments and relentless perseverance. Every property acquired, every tenant relationship nurtured, every hurdle confronted, and every market trend studied became stepping stones toward a greater vision. Through calculated risks and a commitment to continuous learning, I gradually transformed my student loan debt into a flourishing rental property portfolio.

However, as I expanded my real estate assets, I encountered numerous challenges and uncertainties along the way. While I was lucky to benefit from my father's guidance, I recognized a significant gap in resources for amateurs like me who aspired to venture into rental investing but needed more fundamental knowledge to kickstart their journey. Regrettably, I could not find a mentor or a book that would demystify the process for me, providing straightforward explanations of the nuances of investing in rental properties, including its advantages and challenges.

This book aims to fill that gap and provide comprehensive education for individuals completely new to rental property investing. It relies exclusively on my personal experience in real estate to facilitate the generation of passive income. The subject matter covered in this book is what I wish was available to me when I first started investing in rental properties. From understanding the fundamental principles of property selection to mastering the intricacies of financing, property management, and beyond, each chapter provides the essential knowledge needed to begin a journey in investment properties. I have kept the topics relevant and easy to understand, with the hope of making the dream of rental property ownership accessible to everyone, irrespective of their background.

In the final chapter, I have incorporated a comprehensive glossary containing commonly used terms in rental property investing. This addition aims to facilitate a more seamless learning experience and help simplify intricate concepts. My objective is to maintain the book's clarity and educational value by offering precise and understandable definitions, ensuring that novice investors aren't overwhelmed by unfamiliar jargon and technical terminology. Moreover, the extensive glossary serves as a valuable reference tool, enabling readers to swiftly clarify terms and bolster their confidence in real-world scenarios when navigating the complexities of purchasing a rental investment property.

While some topics discussed may seem rudimentary to a seasoned investor, it is essential to reiterate that this book serves as a roadmap for the absolute beginner contemplating investing in rental properties for the very first time. Every successful investor starts with a spark of inspiration, and I am confident that this book will ignite that inspiration for each reader, providing them with the knowledge and motivation to turn their aspirations of passive income into reality. Join me as we embark on a transformative journey toward financial freedom and prosperity through the art and science of building wealth through rental properties.

" It does not matter *when* you start; what matters is *how* you finish. **"**

Let us begin your journey into the world of rental property investing, NOW!!

Dr. Amit Sachdeo

CHAPTER 1

WHAT IS A RENTAL INVESTMENT PROPERTY?

"Buy land, they're not making it anymore."

—*MARK TWAIN, American author and humorist*

An investment is the outlay of money, usually for profit. This can be done through the stock market, a savings account, a certificate of deposit, bonds, mutual funds, retirement plans, real estate, and various business ventures. Of the many investment opportunities out there, real estate stands out as a powerful wealth-building tool that has stood the test of time.

Real estate can be a compelling investment for various reasons. First, it offers the potential for substantial appreciation over time. Historical data indicates that real estate values tend to rise steadily, providing investors with significant returns on their initial investment.

Second, real estate serves as a tangible asset, providing a sense of security and control that may be lacking in other investment vehicles. Unlike stocks or bonds, real estate allows investors to physically see and improve upon their assets, which can be particularly appealing.

Moreover, real estate can generate consistent income through rental properties, offering a reliable cash flow stream that can be used to cover expenses or reinvest. The ability to leverage real estate through mortgage financing enhances the potential for higher returns, as investors can control a more significant asset with a relatively smaller amount of their own capital.

Owning real estate also offers certain tax advantages, including deductions for mortgage interest, property taxes, and depreciation, which can significantly reduce the tax burden on investment income. Since property values and rental income tend to increase over time in line with inflation rates, investing in real estate serves as a hedge against inflation. As inflation erodes the purchasing power of a currency, tangible assets like real estate typically retain or even increase in value. Additionally, rental income often adjusts with inflation, allowing landlords to maintain the property's cash flow and potentially increase rents over time.

A real estate asset purchased with the intention of generating income by renting it out to tenants is called a rental investment property. This type of property can be residential—such as houses, apartments, and condominiums, or commercial—like office buildings, retail spaces, or warehouses. The main goal of a rental investment property is to provide a steady stream of income from rent payments while potentially also appreciating in value over time. This combination of income generation, coupled with appreciation potential, makes rental properties a lucrative choice for investors seeking long-term wealth accumulation and portfolio diversification.

The three key advantages of investing in a rental property are:

1. Cash Flow

2. Property Appreciation

3. Equity

Together, these elements create a robust foundation for long-term wealth accumulation. They provide immediate financial benefits and future investment security, making rental properties a compelling choice for wealth-building strategies.

1.1 Cash Flow

Cash flow is calculated by subtracting all the expenses like a bank loan/mortgage (if any), property taxes, common area utilities (if any), property insurance, etc., from the rent collected every month. If the amount remaining after all deductions from the monthly rent collected is positive, then it is termed as positive cash flow. However, if after deducting all the expenses from the monthly rent collected, the remaining amount is negative, then it is termed negative cash flow. For an investment property to be a lucrative asset and not a liability, it must generate positive cash flow each month.

The illustration below shows an investment property collecting $5,000 in rent each month and $3,500 in monthly expenses. After deducting all the monthly expenses from the rent, the property is left with a profit of $1,500 each month ($5,000 – $3,500 = $1,500). This profit of $1,500 is called positive cash flow.

Table 1. **Cash Flow**

Investment Property	Purchase price of the property	$500,000
Monthly Income	Rent and any additional income generated from the property, e.g., laundry, parking, etc.	$5,000
Monthly Expenses	Mortgage/Loan payment to the bank (if any), property taxes, common area utilities (if any), property insurance, maintenance, management, etc.	$3,500
Monthly Cash Flow	Monthly Income – Monthly Expenses = Monthly Cash Flow	$1,500

1.2 Property Appreciation

If you retain the property over several years, its value will most likely increase over time. This increase in value over time is called property appreciation. Various factors influence property appreciation, including supply and demand dynamics, economic conditions, location, and property-specific characteristics.

A few factors that help a property appreciate in value are:

- **Market Demand:** Property appreciation is driven by demand for real estate in a particular area. When demand exceeds supply, competition among buyers increases, leading to higher prices and property appreciation. Factors such as population growth, job opportunities, lifestyle preferences like walkability, pet friendliness, and cultural and social scene, can influence demand for real estate in a given market.

- **Location:** Location is a critical factor in property appreciation. Properties located in desirable neighborhoods with amenities such as good schools, public transportation, shopping, and recreational facilities tend to appreciate faster than properties in less desirable or declining areas.

- **Economic Conditions:** Economic factors such as inflation, interest rates, employment levels, and economic growth can impact property appreciation. Inflation, for example, can lead to higher property values over time as the purchasing power of currency decreases. Low interest rates can also stimulate demand for real estate, driving property appreciation.

- **Property Improvements:** Property appreciation can be influenced by improvements made to the property. Renovations, upgrades, and additions that enhance the property's appeal, functionality, and aesthetics can increase its market value and contribute to property appreciation.

- **Supply Constraints:** A limited supply of available land and regulatory restrictions on development can constrain housing supply in specific markets, leading to upward pressure on property prices and property appreciation. When demand for housing exceeds supply in a market constrained by land availability and regulatory restrictions, property prices tend to rise. Buyers and renters compete for a limited number of available units, pushing prices upward. This trend is exacerbated in markets where the local economy is strong, job growth is robust, and the desirability of the location remains high. The combination of limited supply and increasing demand often results in property appreciation over time. Homeowners and real estate investors benefit from the appreciation in property values, which can lead to wealth accumulation and increased equity.

- **Market Cycles:** Real estate markets are cyclical and experience periods of expansion, stability, and contraction. Property appreciation rates can vary depending on the phase of the market cycle. During periods of strong economic growth and high demand, property appreciation may accelerate, while during economic downturns or market corrections, property appreciation rates may slow or decline.

Property appreciation is essential for real estate investors as it can contribute to wealth accumulation and financial security over time. However, it is essential to note that property appreciation is not guaranteed, and real estate values can fluctuate based on market conditions and other factors.

1.3 Equity

Equity in real estate is the ownership interest or value that an individual or entity holds in a property. It represents the difference between the property's market value and any outstanding debts or liens against it.

In essence, equity is the portion of the property that the owner truly owns outright and is a measure of the property's net worth and can accrue in several ways:

- **Appreciation:** If the property's market value increases over time due to factors like inflation, improvements in the neighborhood, or enhancements made to the property itself, the owner's equity grows.

- **Improvements and Renovations:** Upgrades or renovations that increase the property's market value can also contribute to equity growth.

- **Outstanding Debt:** The outstanding balance of any mortgage loans or liens on the property represents the amount of money owed by the owner to lenders or creditors. This includes the principal balance of the mortgage loan plus any accrued interest and fees. As the owner pays down any mortgage loan secured against the property, the amount of debt decreases, thereby increasing the owner's equity in the property.

Equity is calculated by subtracting the outstanding debt from the property's market value. Mathematically, it can be expressed as:

$$\text{Equity} = \text{Market Value of Property}^* - \text{Outstanding Mortgage Balance}$$

Property owners can leverage their equity to access financing for various purposes, such as home improvements, debt consolidation, or investment opportunities. This can be done through home equity loans, home equity lines of credit (HELOCs), or cash-out refinancing. Equity is a significant financial asset for investors, as it represents a source of wealth and economic stability. Building equity over time can provide property owners with increased financial security, flexibility, and opportunities for wealth accumulation through real estate ownership.

** The market value of a property is the price at which it would likely sell in the current real estate market. Market value is determined by factors such as location, size, condition, amenities, and comparable sales in the area.*

Table 2. **Property Appreciation and Equity**

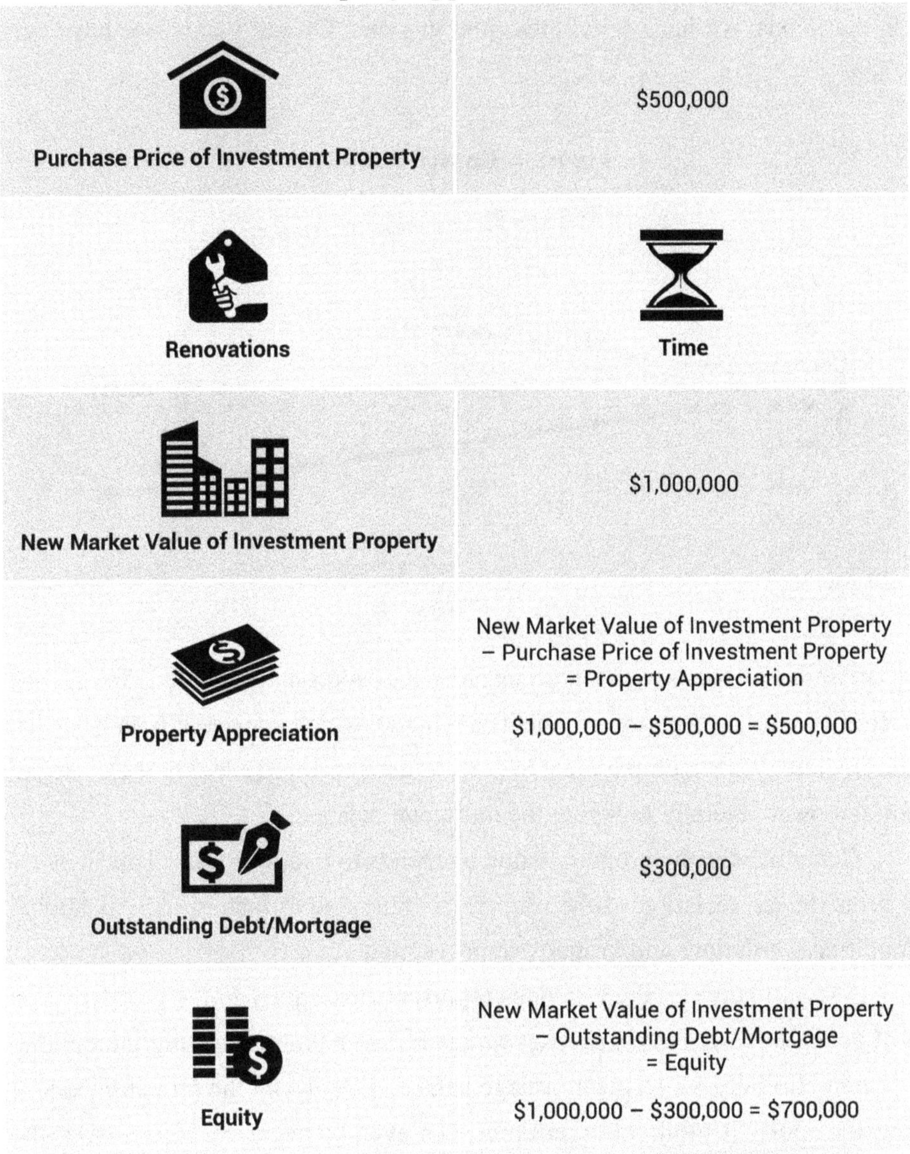

Purchase Price of Investment Property	$500,000
Renovations	**Time**
New Market Value of Investment Property	$1,000,000
Property Appreciation	New Market Value of Investment Property − Purchase Price of Investment Property = Property Appreciation $1,000,000 − $500,000 = $500,000
Outstanding Debt/Mortgage	$300,000
Equity	New Market Value of Investment Property − Outstanding Debt/Mortgage = Equity $1,000,000 − $300,000 = $700,000

Figure 1 below illustrates the equity buildup in a rental property over time. On the x-axis, we have time, measured in years. On the y-axis, we have currency.

Figure 1. **Equity Buildup**

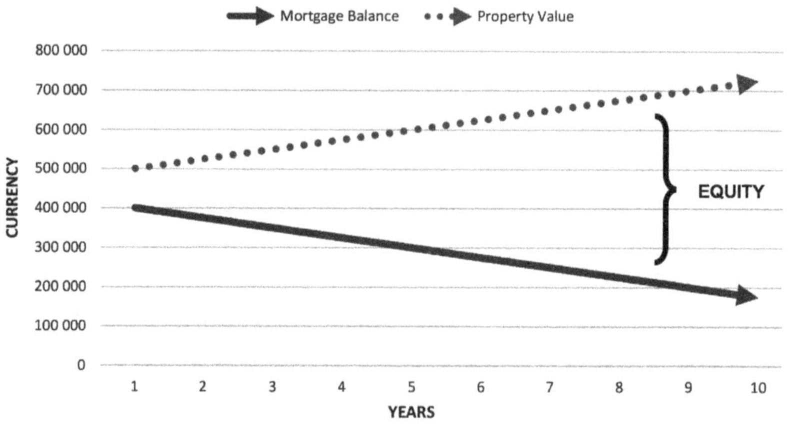

As time progresses, the mortgage balance decreases gradually. This decline occurs as regular mortgage payments are made, which consist of both principal and interest. With each payment, a portion goes toward reducing the principal amount owed, thereby lowering the mortgage balance.

Concurrently, the property value line tends to rise over time. This increase reflects the appreciation of the property's value due to factors such as market conditions, inflation, and property improvements.

The gap between the two lines represents the equity in the property. You will notice how that gap increases gradually over time indicating the buildup of equity. Initially, when the mortgage balance is high and the property value is low, the equity is minimal or, at times, can even be negative. However, as the mortgage balance **decreases** and the property value **increases** over time, the equity in the property grows. Eventually, if the property is held long enough and experiences appreciable value growth while the mortgage balance decreases, the equity in the property can become a significant portion of its total value.

The combination of positive cash flow, property appreciation, and equity buildup over time can make an investment rental property highly lucrative, providing immediate cash flow and long-term wealth accumulation. Additionally, factors such as thorough due diligence in property selection, prudent property management, and staying informed about local market trends can further enhance the profitability of rental property investments.

Here are a few case studies showcasing real-life examples of real estate investing:

Case Study 1: THE FIX-AND-FLIP SUCCESS STORY

- » ***Background:*** Richard, an experienced real estate investor, purchased a distressed property in a desirable neighborhood at a below-market price. The property required significant renovations but had excellent potential for appreciation.

- » ***Strategy:*** Richard renovated the property, focusing on high-impact upgrades such as modernizing the kitchen and bathrooms, refinishing hardwood floors, and enhancing curb appeal. He marketed the property aggressively, leveraging professional staging and photography to attract potential buyers.

- » ***Outcome:*** After completing the renovations, Richard sold the property for a substantial profit, capitalizing on the increased market value and demand for turnkey homes in the area.

- » ***Lesson Learned:*** Successful fix-and-flip projects require careful planning, accurate cost estimation, and a keen understanding of market trends. It is crucial to focus on improvements that provide the highest return on investment and have a solid exit strategy.

Case Study 2: THE CASH FLOW RENTAL PROPERTY

- » ***Background:*** Karen, a first-time investor, purchased a multi-family property in a growing rental market. The property offered multiple rental units, providing diversified income streams and potential for cash flow.

» **Strategy:** Karen conducted thorough market research to identify an area with strong rental demand and favorable demographics. She purchased the property with a conventional mortgage, aiming to generate positive cash flow after covering expenses such as mortgage payments, taxes, insurance, and maintenance.

» **Outcome:** Karen successfully rented out all units at market rates, exceeding her cash flow projections. With careful property management and tenant screening, she maintained high occupancy rates and minimized vacancies, resulting in steady rental income.

» **Lesson Learned:** Cash flow rental properties can provide consistent returns and long-term wealth accumulation. However, it is essential to choose properties in stable markets with strong rental demand and to manage them effectively to maximize profitability.

Case Study 3: THE LONG-TERM APPRECIATION INVESTMENT

» **Background:** James, a seasoned investor, purchased a residential property in an up-and-coming neighborhood with potential for long-term appreciation. While the property's rental income initially covered expenses, James's primary focus was on capital appreciation over time.

» **Strategy:** James held onto the property for several years, monitoring market trends and making strategic improvements to enhance its value. He invested in neighborhood revitalization efforts, such as community amenities and infrastructure upgrades, to attract more buyers and increase property values.

» **Outcome:** Over the years, the property's value appreciated significantly, outperforming the market average. James eventually sold the property for a substantial profit, realizing his investment goals and achieving impressive returns on his initial investment.

» **Lesson Learned:** Investing for long-term appreciation requires patience, vision, and a thorough understanding of market dynamics. It is essential to identify emerging neighborhoods with growth potential and to stay informed about economic trends and development projects that can impact property values over time.

These case studies illustrate the diverse strategies and outcomes in real estate investing, emphasizing the importance of research, planning, and execution in achieving success. Whether focusing on fix-and-flip projects, cash flow rental properties, or long-term appreciation investments, investors can learn valuable lessons from real-life examples to make their own investment decisions.

Advantages of a rental investment property:

- Steady passive income.
- Tangible asset.
- Property appreciation.
- Leverage.
- Hedge against inflation.
- Diversification.
- Tax benefits.
- Control and flexibility.
- Long-term wealth accumulation.
- Equity building.

CHAPTER 2
TYPES OF RENTAL PROPERTIES

"Landlords grow rich in their sleep."

—JOHN STUART MILL, British philosopher and economist

Understanding the diverse array of property types is paramount in the realm of rental properties. There are several types of rental investment properties that individuals can consider when building their real estate portfolio. Each category offers its unique advantages, challenges, and potential for returns, shaping the landscape of one's investment journey. Some of the most common types of rental properties are:

- **Residential Rental Properties:** These include single-family homes, condominiums, townhouses, duplexes, triplexes, and apartment buildings that are rented out to tenants. Residential properties typically provide a steady stream of rental income and can appreciate in value over time.

- **Commercial Properties:** Commercial real estate encompasses a wide range of property types, including office buildings, retail spaces, industrial warehouses, and mixed-use developments. Commercial properties often offer higher rental yields but may require larger initial investments and come with additional complexities such as longer leasing cycles and higher maintenance costs.

- **NNN Properties:** An "NNN" investment property refers to a commercial real estate investment where the tenant is responsible for paying the net amount of property taxes, insurance, and maintenance costs, in addition to the base rent. The term "NNN" stands for "Triple-Net Lease," indicating that the tenant bears the burden of these additional expenses, beyond just the base rent. This type of arrangement is common in commercial real estate, particularly with long-term leases involving properties such as retail spaces, office buildings, or industrial facilities.

- **Vacation Rentals:** Vacation rental properties, such as beach houses, cabins, or condos in tourist destinations, are rented out to vacationers on a short-term basis. While vacation rentals can generate higher rental income during peak seasons, they may also require more hands-on management and incur higher turnover costs.

- **Multi-family Properties:** Multi-family properties, such as apartment complexes or multi-unit buildings, contain multiple residential units within a single structure. Investing in multi-family properties can diversify risk by spreading rental income across multiple units and tenants.

- **Mixed-Use Properties:** Mixed-use properties combine residential and commercial spaces within the same building or development. For example, a building may have retail or office space on the ground floor and residential units on the upper floors. Mixed-use properties can provide multiple streams of income and potentially attract a diverse range of tenants.

- **Industrial Properties:** Industrial real estate includes warehouses, distribution centers, manufacturing facilities, and flex spaces. Industrial properties are often leased to businesses for storage, distribution, or production purposes and can offer stable long-term rental income.

- **Specialized Properties:** Some investors may choose to invest in specialized types of properties, such as senior housing, student housing, healthcare facilities, or self-storage facilities. These properties cater to specific demographics or needs and may offer unique investment opportunities.

- **Real Estate Investment Trusts (REITs):** REITs are companies that own, operate, or finance income-generating real estate across various sectors. Investing in REITs allows individuals to gain exposure to real estate markets without directly owning physical properties. REITs typically distribute a portion of their income to shareholders in the form of dividends.

From the steadfast stability of single-family homes to the dynamic potential of commercial spaces, each property type presents its unique blend of advantages and challenges. Single-family homes offer simplicity and familiarity, making them an ideal entry point for novice investors seeking steady rental income. Conversely, multi-unit properties provide scalability and diversification, albeit with added management complexity. Commercial properties, with their potential for higher returns and longer leases, cater to investors with a penchant for risk and a strategic vision for long-term growth.

Investors can also choose to have either a long-term or a short-term rental property based on factors such as their financial goals, risk tolerance, location, property type, and management preferences. Both types of investments can offer opportunities for income and appreciation, but they come with different considerations and challenges.

Long-term rental properties are leased to tenants for an extended period, typically six months or longer. The primary goal of long-term rental investments is to generate steady, predictable rental income over an extended period. Examples include single-family homes, apartments, and condominiums rented out to tenants on yearly leases. Long-term rental properties often provide stable cash flow and may appreciate in value over time.

Table 3. **Advantages and Disadvantages of a Long-Term Rental Property**

ADVANTAGES OF A LONG-TERM RENTAL PROPERTY	DISADVANTAGES OF A LONG-TERM RENTAL PROPERTY
Stable Income: Long-term rental properties typically provide a stable, consistent income stream since tenants sign leases for extended periods, such as six months or a year.	**Limited Income Potential:** Long-term rentals typically generate lower rental income compared to short-term rentals, especially in high-demand tourist areas.
Reduced Turnover Costs: With longer lease terms, you will likely have fewer vacancies and turnover costs associated with finding new tenants and preparing the property between occupants.	**Less Flexibility:** You have less flexibility to adjust rental rates and terms frequently since tenants are locked into lease agreements for longer periods.
Predictable Expenses: You can more accurately predict expenses such as maintenance, utilities, and property management fees since they tend to be more consistent with long-term rentals.	**Tenant Issues:** Dealing with problematic tenants, such as late payments, property damage, or lease violations, can be more challenging in long-term rentals.
Lower Time Commitment: Long-term rentals generally require less time and effort to manage compared to short-term rentals since you're dealing with fewer turnover events and guest interactions.	**Market Changes:** Changes in the local rental market or economic conditions can impact long-term rental demand and rental rates over time.

Short-term rental properties, also known as vacation rentals or Airbnb properties, involve renting out a property for a brief period, usually days or weeks, rather than months or years. These properties are popular in tourist destinations or areas with high demand for temporary accommodation. Short-term rentals can yield higher rental income compared to long-term rentals, especially during peak seasons, but they may also come with higher operating costs, such as cleaning fees and property management expenses. Examples include vacation homes, cottages, and apartments rented out to travelers on platforms like Airbnb or VRBO. Tables 3 and 4 outline some key advantages and disadvantages of long-term and short-term rental properties.

Table 4. **Advantages and Disadvantages of a Short-Term Rental Property**

ADVANTAGES OF A SHORT-TERM RENTAL PROPERTY	DISADVANTAGES OF A SHORT-TERM RENTAL PROPERTY
Higher Income Potential: Short-term rentals often command higher nightly rates, especially in popular tourist destinations or during peak seasons, resulting in potentially higher overall income.	**High Turnover and Vacancy Rates:** Short-term rentals typically experience higher turnover and vacancy rates, leading to more frequent cleaning, maintenance, and downtime between guests.
Flexibility: You have the flexibility to use the property for personal use when it's not booked by guests, allowing you to enjoy your property while still generating income.	**Intensive Management:** Managing short-term rentals requires more time and effort, including coordinating check-ins/outs, responding to guest inquiries and issues promptly, and maintaining the property to high standards.
Dynamic Pricing: You can adjust nightly rates based on demand, seasonality, and events, maximizing income during peak periods.	**Regulatory Challenges:** Short-term rentals may be subject to stricter regulations, zoning laws, and homeowner association rules compared to long-term rentals, requiring compliance efforts and potential legal risks.
Meeting New People: Hosting guests from different parts of the world can be a rewarding experience, providing opportunities for cultural exchange and making new connections.	**Seasonal Demand:** Short-term rental income can be highly dependent on seasonal fluctuations and tourism trends, resulting in less predictable income compared to long-term rentals. In some areas, the market may be saturated with Airbnb listings, making it challenging to attract guests and maintain consistent bookings.
Additional Income: Renting out your property on Airbnb can generate extra income, which can be particularly beneficial if you have a spare room or property that is not in use all the time.	**Damage and Security Concerns:** There is always a risk of damage to your property by guests, which could result in repair costs and potential downtime for renting. Hosting strangers in your property can also raise security concerns, both for your belongings and for the safety of your guests.
Tax Benefits: Depending on your location and circumstances, you may be eligible for certain tax deductions related to operating a rental property.	**Management and Maintenance:** Managing an Airbnb property requires time and effort, including cleaning between guests, managing bookings, and addressing maintenance issues promptly.

Here are two case studies of long-term and short-term rental properties:

Case Study 1: LONG-TERM RENTAL PROPERTY

» *Background:* David, an investor, purchased a residential property in a suburban neighborhood with the intention of renting it out on a long-term basis. He aimed to generate steady cash flow and build equity through rental income and property appreciation.

» *Strategy:* David conducted market research to identify neighborhoods with strong rental demand and favorable rental yield potential. He renovated the property to attract quality tenants and priced the rent competitively to ensure consistent occupancy.

» *Outcome:* The long-term rental property provided David with stable rental income and minimal vacancies due to its desirable location and well-maintained condition. Over time, the property appreciated in value, further enhancing David's return on investment.

» *Lessons Learned:* David learned the importance of location, property condition, and tenant selection in long-term rental investments. He also realized the benefits of steady cash flow and equity buildup associated with long-term rental properties.

Case Study 2: SHORT-TERM RENTAL PROPERTY

» *Background:* Emily, an investor, purchased a vacation rental property in a popular tourist destination near the beach. She aimed to capitalize on the high demand for short-term accommodation among vacationers.

» *Strategy:* Emily furnished the property attractively, highlighting its proximity to local attractions and amenities. She listed the property on various short-term rental platforms and implemented dynamic pricing strategies to maximize occupancy and rental income during peak seasons

» **Outcome:** The vacation rental property generated significant rental income during peak seasons, often surpassing the income potential of long-term rentals. However, Emily faced challenges during off-peak seasons, such as increased vacancy rates and fluctuating demand.

» **Lessons Learned:** Emily learned the importance of seasonality, pricing strategy, and property management in short-term rental investments. She also realized the need for flexibility and contingency plans to navigate fluctuations in demand and occupancy.

These case studies illustrate the different strategies, outcomes, and lessons learned in long-term and short-term rental property investments, highlighting the importance of market research, property management, and adaptability in maximizing returns and mitigating risks. It is essential to evaluate your investment goals, risk tolerance, market conditions, and personal preferences to determine which option aligns best with your objectives. Each type of property comes with its own set of advantages, risks, and considerations, so it's essential to conduct thorough research and consider your investment goals and risk tolerance before making any investment decisions.

There is no one-size-fits-all approach to the type of rental investment property. Investors must embrace flexibility, foresight, and a willingness to adapt their strategies to evolving market conditions and investment objectives. Whether aiming for cash flow, appreciation, or a combination of both, one must carefully assess the local market conditions, economic trends, and tenant demographics to make informed decisions. It is important to align investment goals, risk tolerance, and market dynamics with the choice of rental property type.

Types of rental properties:

- Residential properties: Single-family homes and multi-family properties.
- Commercial properties: Office buildings and retail properties.
- Vacation/Short-term Rental properties: Airbnb and VRBO.
- Mixed-use properties: Combine both residential and commercial units.
- Specialized properties: Student housing, senior housing, and affordable housing.

CHAPTER 3

PARTNERSHIPS IN RENTAL INVESTMENT PROPERTIES

"Every person who invests in well-selected real estate
in a growing section of a prosperous community adopts the surest
and safest method of becoming independent,
for real estate is the basis of wealth."

—THEODORE ROOSEVELT, former President of the United States

Depending on your financial goals, risk tolerance, expertise, and available resources, becoming a partner in a real estate investment can be a beneficial move under various circumstances. A real estate partnership is a business arrangement in which two or more individuals or entities come together to jointly own, manage, and invest in real estate properties. Partnerships are formed to leverage each partner's resources, expertise, and capital to pursue common real estate investment goals. Some reasons why one might consider a partnership are:

- **Limited Capital:** If you have limited capital to invest but want to access larger real estate opportunities, partnering with others allows you to pool resources and participate in projects that would otherwise be out of reach.

- **Limited Experience:** Partnering with individuals or entities who have expertise and experience in real estate investing can provide valuable mentorship and guidance, especially if you're new to the industry. Learning from experienced partners can help mitigate risks and increase the likelihood of success.

- **Risk Mitigation:** Real estate investments come with inherent risks, including market fluctuations, property maintenance issues, and regulatory changes. Partnering with others spreads the risk across multiple investors, reducing individual exposure and potential losses.

- **Access to Deals:** Partnerships can provide access to deals and opportunities that may not be available to individual investors. Networking with other investors and industry professionals can lead to new investment opportunities and potential joint ventures.

- **Diversification:** Partnering in real estate investments allows you to diversify your portfolio across different properties, asset classes, and geographic locations. Diversification helps spread risk and can enhance overall portfolio stability.

- **Shared Expertise:** Partnering with individuals who bring complementary skills and expertise to the table can enhance the success of the investment. For example, partnering with someone who has expertise in property management, finance, or construction can add value to the partnership.

- **Scale and Efficiency:** By partnering with others, you can achieve economies of scale and operational efficiencies in managing real estate investments. Shared resources, such as property management services, maintenance costs, and administrative tasks, can lead to cost savings and increased profitability.

- **Tax Benefits:** Certain partnership structures, such as limited partnerships and REITs, offer tax advantages, including pass-through taxation and deductions for depreciation and interest expenses, which can enhance overall investment returns.

Partnerships are a common structure for real estate ventures because they allow multiple parties to combine their resources, expertise, and capital to pursue opportunities that may be beyond the reach of any one partner individually, so long as the relationship and understanding between the partners remain cordial. Some common types of partnerships in real estate investing are:

- **General Partnership (GP):** In a general partnership, all partners share equal responsibility for the management and liabilities of the investment. Decisions are typically made jointly, and profits are divided according to the partnership agreement.

- **Limited Partnership (LP):** Limited partnerships have two types of partners: general partners and limited partners. General partners manage the investment and are liable for its debts, while limited partners contribute capital and have limited liability. Limited partners usually have no involvement in the day-to-day operations.

- **Limited Liability Partnership (LLP):** LLPs are similar to general partnerships but with the added benefit of limited liability protection for all partners. This means that each partner is not personally liable for the debts and obligations of the partnership.

- **Joint Venture (JV):** Joint ventures are formed for a specific project or investment opportunity. Partners come together to pool resources, share expertise, and spread risks associated with the venture. Joint ventures can be structured in various ways depending on the needs and objectives of the partners.

- **Real Estate Investment Trust (REIT):** REITs are companies that own, operate, or finance income-producing real estate across a range of property sectors. They offer investors the opportunity to invest in real estate without directly owning or managing properties. REITs are traded on major stock exchanges and must distribute at least 90% of their taxable income to shareholders in the form of dividends.

- **Syndication:** Real estate syndication involves pooling funds from multiple investors to acquire or develop a property. A syndicator or sponsor manages the investment and typically receives a share of the profits in exchange for their expertise and effort. Investors can participate as limited partners in the syndication.

- **Real Estate Crowdfunding:** Crowdfunding platforms enable individuals to invest in real estate projects with relatively small amounts of capital. Investors can browse through various investment opportunities and choose projects that align with their investment goals. Crowdfunding platforms may operate under different structures, including equity crowdfunding and debt crowdfunding, that allow pooling capital from many individual investors, each contributing a relatively small amount, to collectively fund the purchase, renovation, and management of rental properties.

Each partnership structure has its advantages and disadvantages in terms of liability, management control, tax implications, and investment flexibility. It is crucial for partners to have a clear understanding of their roles, responsibilities, and expectations, which are typically outlined in a partnership agreement. This agreement specifies the terms of the partnership, including profit-sharing arrangements, decision-making processes, exit strategies, dispute-resolution mechanisms, etc. Ultimately, while partnering in rental property investment can offer numerous benefits, it is crucial to thoroughly assess compatibility and ensure that the partnership aligns with your long-term objectives and values.

Forming a partnership for a rental investment property involves several key steps and considerations to ensure a smooth and successful collaboration. Outlined below is a guide on how to form such a partnership and what precautions to take to stay safe.

Here are the major steps when forming a partnership for a rental investment property:

1. **Identify Potential Partners:**
   - Look for partners who share similar investment goals, risk tolerance, and time horizons.
   - Consider potential partners' financial stability, experience in real estate, and complementary skills.

2. **Define the Partnership Structure**:
   - Decide on the type of partnership: general partnership (GP), limited partnership (LP), or limited liability company (LLC).
   - An LLC is often preferred for real estate investments due to its liability protection and flexible management structure.
3. **Outline Roles and Responsibilities**:
   - Clearly define each partner's roles, responsibilities, and contributions (financial, managerial, operational).
   - Determine how decisions will be made and who will handle day-to-day management.
4. **Draft a Partnership Agreement**:
   - Work with a real estate attorney to draft a comprehensive partnership agreement.
   - Include details on capital contributions, profit and loss distribution, decision-making processes, dispute resolution, exit strategies, and procedures for adding or removing partners.
5. **Secure Financing**:
   - Determine how the property will be financed (partner contributions, bank loans, etc.).
   - Ensure all partners understand their financial obligations and the impact on their personal credit.
6. **Conduct Due Diligence**:
   - Perform thorough due diligence on the property, including inspections, appraisals, and market analysis.
   - Ensure all partners are fully informed about the property's condition, location, and potential return on investment.
7. **Close the Deal**:
   - Purchase the property in the name of the partnership or LLC.
   - Ensure all legal documents and financing are properly executed and recorded.

While real estate partnerships offer the potential for increased capital, expertise, and diversification, they also come with risks and challenges that investors should carefully consider before entering into a partnership agreement. An attorney friend once told me, "It's not a problem until there is a problem." That phrase has stuck with me ever since. Not all partnerships have issues, but there have been many times when there has been legal or financial trouble for one of the partners, a difference of opinion between partners, or there has been alleged financial mismanagement by one of the partners causing the business or investment to suffer.

It can, at times, often be better to get a smaller property by yourself than buy something bigger with a partner. As a sole owner, you have full control and the liberty to make all decisions, however big or small, by yourself. You decide what property to buy, you decide on the tenants, you decide who manages the property, you make the decisions on any capital improvements, you decide if you want to keep or sell the property and who to will it to in your estate plans.

Here are some precautions one must keep in mind when forming a partnership:

1. **Legal Protection**:
   - Form an LLC to protect partners' personal assets from liabilities related to the property.
   - Ensure the partnership agreement is legally binding and covers all possible scenarios.

2. **Clear Communication**:
   - Maintain open and honest communication with partners.
   - Hold regular meetings to discuss property performance, financial status, and any issues or concerns.

3. **Due Diligence on Partners**:
   - Conduct background checks and verify the financial stability of potential partners.
   - Ensure all partners have a good track record and a solid understanding of real estate investing.

4. **Insurance**:
   - Obtain adequate property and liability insurance to protect against potential losses and legal claims.
   - Consider additional insurance for the partnership itself, such as errors and omissions insurance.

5. **Financial Transparency**:
   - Keep detailed financial records and provide regular reports to all partners.
   - Use accounting software to track income, expenses, and distributions accurately.

6. **Exit Strategy**:
   - Include clear exit strategies in the partnership agreement, such as buy-sell provisions and procedures for dissolving the partnership.
   - Discuss and agree on these strategies upfront to avoid conflicts later.

7. **Consult Professionals**:
   - Seek advice from real estate attorneys, accountants, and financial advisors to ensure the partnership is structured correctly and complies with all legal and tax requirements.
   - Regularly consult these professionals to stay updated on any changes in laws or regulations that may affect the partnership.

By following these steps and taking necessary precautions, you can form a successful and secure partnership for rental property investing. Proper planning, clear agreements, and diligent management are key to avoiding disputes and ensuring a profitable venture. Table 5 outlines some key advantages and disadvantages of a partnership in rental property investing.

Table 5. **Advantages and Disadvantages of a Partnership**

ADVANTAGES OF A PARTNERSHIP	DISADVANTAGES OF A PARTNERSHIP
Access to Capital: Partnerships allow investors to pool their financial resources, making it easier to finance larger real estate deals that may be beyond the reach of any single investor.	**Shared Decision-Making**: In partnerships, decisions must be made collectively, which can sometimes lead to disagreements or conflicts among partners. This can slow down the decision-making process and hinder the partnership's ability to capitalize on opportunities quickly.
Diversification: Partnerships enable investors to spread their risk across multiple properties or projects, reducing the impact of any single investment's performance on their overall portfolio.	**Potential for Disputes**: Disputes may arise over issues such as property management, financial management, profit distribution, and exit strategies. Without clear communication and a well-defined partnership agreement, disagreements can escalate and disrupt the partnership.
Shared Expertise: Partnerships often bring together individuals with diverse skills, knowledge, and experience in real estate investing, property management, finance, or other relevant areas. This shared expertise can enhance decision-making and improve the overall success of the partnership.	**Profit Sharing**: Partnerships require sharing profits with other investors, which means that each partner receives a portion of the returns based on their ownership stake. This can dilute individual returns compared to investing independently in a property.
Increased Opportunities: By combining resources and networks, partnerships can access a broader range of real estate opportunities, including off-market deals, distressed properties, or development projects.	**Liability Exposure**: In general partnerships, all partners have unlimited personal liability for the debts and obligations of the partnership. Even in limited partnerships, general partners have unlimited liability, while limited partners' liability is typically limited to their investment amount.
Tax Benefits: Depending on the partnership structure and tax regulations, investors may benefit from tax advantages such as pass-through taxation, depreciation deductions, or the ability to defer capital gains through 1031 exchanges.	**Dependency on Partners**: Partnerships rely on the contributions and cooperation of all partners. If one partner fails to fulfill their obligations or withdraws from the partnership unexpectedly, it can disrupt operations and potentially jeopardize the success of the investment.
Efficiency: Partnerships can achieve economies of scale and operational efficiencies in managing real estate investments. Shared resources, such as property management services, maintenance costs, and administrative tasks, can lead to cost savings and increased profitability.	**Complexity and Administration**: Real estate partnerships require careful planning, documentation, and ongoing management. Setting up and maintaining a partnership involves legal and administrative complexities, including drafting partnership agreements, managing finances, and complying with regulatory requirements.

In the end, the choice to engage in a partnership for your rental property investment should correspond with your future goals, financial resources, and willingness to jointly own and make decisions. Seeking guidance from experts in finance, law, and real estate can offer valuable perspectives to guide your decision-making journey.

Here are a couple of case studies showcasing successful and failed partnerships in rental property investing:

Case Study 1: SUCCESSFUL PARTNERSHIP

» *Background:* Ray and Debbie, two friends with complementary skills and resources, decided to pool their resources to invest in rental properties. Ray had experience in real estate acquisitions and property management, while Debbie had a background in finance and a strong network of potential investors.

» *Strategy:* Ray and Debbie identified a market with strong rental demand and favorable economic indicators. They decided to invest in a multi-family property in a growing urban area. Ray handled property acquisition, renovations, and day-to-day management, while Debbie secured financing through her investor network and managed the financial aspects of the investment.

» *Outcome:* The partnership proved to be highly successful. Ray's expertise in property management ensured that the rental units were well-maintained and attractively priced, leading to high occupancy rates and steady rental income. Debbie's ability to secure financing at favorable terms allowed the partnership to leverage their capital efficiently and expand their portfolio over time.

» *Lesson Learned:* This case study highlights the benefits of partnerships in rental property investing, particularly when partners bring complementary skills and resources to the table. By combining their expertise and networks, Ray and Debbie were able to capitalize on investment opportunities and achieve greater success together than they could have individually.

Case Study 2: FAILED PARTNERSHIP

» **Background:** Alex and Ryan, two childhood friends, decided to invest in rental properties together to capitalize on the booming real estate market in their area. Alex had experience in property management, while Ryan had a background in sales and marketing.

» **Strategy:** Alex and Ryan identified a duplex property in a desirable neighborhood and saw an opportunity to generate rental income by converting it into two separate rental units. They agreed to split the responsibilities, with Alex handling property maintenance and tenant relations, while Ryan focused on marketing and finding tenants.

» **Outcome:** Initially, the partnership seemed promising, and Alex and Ryan successfully renovated the duplex and found tenants for both units. However, conflicts began to arise when it came to decision-making and financial management. Alex felt that Ryan was not pulling his weight in terms of finding tenants and contributing to property expenses, while Ryan believed Alex was too controlling and reluctant to listen to his input. The disagreements between Alex and Ryan escalated, leading to strained communication and ultimately a breakdown in the partnership. Ryan stopped actively participating in property management, leaving Alex to handle everything on his own. This resulted in neglect of the property, delays in addressing maintenance issues, and difficulty finding new tenants when the existing ones moved out.

» **Lesson Learned:** This case study highlights the importance of clear communication, mutual respect, and aligned goals in partnerships. Alex and Ryan's failure to effectively communicate and resolve conflicts led to the deterioration of their partnership and the performance of the rental property. It underscores the need for partners to establish clear expectations, define roles and responsibilities, and address issues promptly to ensure the success of their investment endeavors.

Advantages and disadvantages of partnerships in an investment property:

ADVANTAGES:

- Shared financial burden.
- Combined expertise and resources.
- Potential for diversified portfolio.
- Flexibility in decision-making.
- Tax benefits pass through to partners.

DISADVANTAGES:

- Shared profits and decision-making.
- Potential for disagreements and conflicts.
- Personal liability for debts and obligations.
- Limited access to capital compared to corporations.
- Dependency on partner's actions and decisions.

CHAPTER 4

TAX INCENTIVES FOR RENTAL PROPERTIES

"The major fortunes in America have been made in land."

—JOHN D. ROCKEFELLER, American business magnate and philanthropist

Owning a rental property offers several tax incentives that can help reduce taxable income and maximize returns for property owners. Understanding the tax implications of rental income, expenses, deductions, and strategies can help property owners maximize their profits and minimize their tax liabilities, although it is important to consult with a tax professional for personalized advice. Some common tax benefits associated with owning rental properties are:

- **Mortgage Interest Deduction:** Property owners can deduct mortgage interest paid on loans used to acquire, improve, or refinance rental investment properties. This deduction can significantly reduce taxable income and lower overall tax liability.

- **Property Tax Deduction:** Property owners can deduct property taxes paid on rental investment properties as an operating expense. This deduction helps offset the cost of property taxes and reduce taxable income.

- **Depreciation Deduction:** Rental investment property owners can claim depreciation deductions for the gradual wear and tear of the property over time. Depreciation allows property owners to deduct a portion of the property's cost each year over its useful life, providing substantial tax benefits and lowering taxable income. This is perhaps one of the most significant tax benefits of owning a rental property. Depreciation deductions can offset rental income, reduce taxable income, and increase cash flow without requiring any actual expenditure.

- **Operating Expenses Deduction:** Property owners can deduct a wide range of operating expenses associated with owning and operating rental investment properties. These may include property management fees, maintenance and repairs, utilities, insurance premiums, advertising costs, homeowner association fees, and other eligible expenses.

- **Travel and Transportation Deduction:** Property owners may be able to deduct travel and transportation expenses related to managing their rental properties, such as mileage, vehicle expenses, and travel costs for property inspections, meetings with tenants, or property maintenance activities.

- **Repairs and Maintenance Deduction:** Property owners can deduct expenses for repairs and maintenance necessary to keep the rental property in good operating condition. This includes costs for routine maintenance, minor repairs, and upkeep of the property.

- **Professional Services Deduction:** Property owners can deduct expenses for professional services related to managing rental properties, such as legal fees, accounting fees, property management fees, and other professional services necessary for property operations.

- **Capital Improvements Depreciation:** While the cost of capital improvements (such as renovations or major repairs) cannot be deducted immediately, it can be depreciated over time, providing tax benefits in subsequent years.

- **Passive Activity Losses Deduction:** Property owners may be able to deduct passive activity losses from rental real estate investments against other passive income or offsetting ordinary income, subject to certain limitations and passive activity loss rules.

- **Qualified Business Income Deduction (QBI):** Rental real estate activities may qualify for the QBI deduction under certain circumstances. This deduction allows eligible taxpayers to deduct up to 20% of their QBI from pass-through entities, including rental income.

- **Section 1031 Exchange:** Through a 1031 exchange, property owners can defer capital gains taxes by exchanging one rental investment property for another of equal or greater value, as long as certain requirements are met.

It is essential for rental property owners to keep accurate records of income and expenses related to their properties and consult with a tax advisor or accountant to maximize available deductions, comply with tax laws, and optimize tax strategies based on their individual circumstances. Here are some examples of real-life case studies showing the tax benefits of investing in rental properties:

Case Study 1: DEPRECIATION DEDUCTIONS

» *Investor Profile:*
Name: Jennifer
Age: 45
Investment Experience: Moderate in real estate
Financial Goal: Maximize tax savings through rental property investments

» *Property:*
Purchase Price: $300,000
Property Type: Single-family rental
Condition: Good, minor renovations needed

» **Depreciation:** Jennifer leveraged the Internal Revenue Service's (IRS) Modified Accelerated Cost Recovery System (MACRS), which allows the capitalized cost of an asset to be recovered over a specified period via annual deductions. This allowed her to depreciate the property over 27.5 years. She allocated $270,000 (excluding land value) for depreciation.

» **Annual depreciation deduction:**
$270,000 / 27.5 = $9,818

» **Additional Deductions:**
Mortgage interest
Property taxes
Maintenance and repairs

» **Annual Tax Savings:**
Depreciation: $9,818
Mortgage Interest: $6,000
Property Taxes: $3,000
Maintenance/Repairs: $2,000
Total Deductions: $20,818

» **Tax Impact:** Jennifer's effective taxable rental income was reduced from $18,000 to $2,818, resulting in significant tax savings and even a potential carryover loss to offset future income.

» **Lesson Learned:** Depreciation is a powerful tool for reducing taxable income on rental properties. By fully leveraging tax deductions, investors can significantly decrease their tax liability and enhance cash flow.

Case Study 2: 1031 EXCHANGE

» **Investor Profile:**
Name: Robert
Age: 50
Investment Experience: Extensive in real estate
Financial Goal: Defer capital gains taxes while upgrading properties

» ***Property:***
Initial Property: Single-family house
Purchase Price: $400,000
Sale Price: $600,000
Profit From Sale: $200,000 (Sale Price − Purchase Price)

» ***Strategy:***
1031 Exchange: Robert used a 1031 Exchange, which allows real estate investors to swap one investment property for another and defer capital gains taxes. He deferred capital gains taxes by reinvesting the proceeds from the sale of his single-family home into a more valuable property.

» ***Replacement Property:***
Purchase Price: $900,000
Property Type: Two-family house

» ***Timeline:***
Identified replacement property within 45 days
Closed on the new property within 180 days

» ***Tax Deferral:*** Robert deferred capital gains taxes on the $200,000 profit from the sale, allowing him to reinvest the full amount into the new property.

» ***Increased Cash Flow:*** The two-family house generated significantly higher rental income, enhancing his overall cash flow.

» ***Lesson Learned:*** A 1031 Exchange is an effective strategy for deferring capital gains taxes and leveraging equity to acquire higher-value properties, thereby increasing rental income and long-term investment growth.

Case Study 3: TAX-FREE REFINANCING

» ***Investor Profile:***
Name: Lisa
Age: 38
Investment Experience: Beginner in real estate
Financial Goal: Access equity without selling property and incurring taxes

» **Property:**
Purchase Price: $200,000
Current Value: $300,000

» **Existing Loan Terms:**
Loan Amount: $160,000
Interest Rate: 3.5%
Monthly Payment: $718

» **Refinancing:** Lisa refinanced her rental property to access $80,000 of its increased equity without triggering a taxable event.

» **New Loan Terms:**
Loan Amount: $240,000 (80% of current value)
Interest Rate: 3.5%
Monthly Payment: $1,078

» **Use of Funds:** Invested the $80,000 into another rental property to further increase her rental portfolio.

» **Tax-Free Equity:** Lisa accessed $80,000 of equity tax-free, avoiding capital gains taxes and using the funds to expand her investment portfolio.

» **Increased Portfolio:** With the additional rental property, Lisa increased her monthly rental income and potential for future appreciation.

» **Lesson Learned:** Refinancing can be a strategic way to access property equity tax-free. It allows investors to reinvest in additional properties and grow their rental portfolio without incurring immediate tax liabilities.

Case Study 4: HOME OFFICE DEDUCTION

» **Investor Profile:**
Name: Mark
Age: 32
Investment Experience: Minimal, first rental property

» **Financial Goal:** Maximize tax savings through home office deduction

» ***Property:***
Purchase Price: $250,000
Property Type: Single-family rental

» ***Home Office Deduction:*** Mark dedicated 10% of his home for rental property management activities. He calculated the home office deduction based on the percentage of home expenses attributable to the office space.

» ***Eligible Expenses:***
Mortgage interest
Property taxes
Utilities
Home insurance

» ***Calculation:***
Total Home Expenses: $20,000
Home Office Deduction: 10% of $20,000 = $2,000

» ***Outcome:*** Tax Savings: Mark reduced his taxable rental income by $2,000 due to the home office deduction, lowering his overall tax liability.

» ***Efficient Management:*** The home office facilitated better property management and organization, enhancing operational efficiency.

» ***Lesson Learned:*** Utilizing the home office deduction for rental property management can provide significant tax savings. Proper documentation and calculation are essential to maximize this benefit and ensure compliance with IRS regulations.

The above case studies highlight how different tax benefits can be leveraged in rental property investing to maximize returns and reduce tax liabilities. The tax landscape can be complex, so it is essential for real estate investors to work closely with knowledgeable tax professionals or financial advisors familiar with real estate taxation laws to maximize the benefits of these incentives and ensure compliance with relevant regulations. Additionally, tax laws and regulations can vary by jurisdiction and may change over time, so investors should stay informed about any updates or changes that could affect their tax liability.

Tax benefits of investing in rental properties:

- Mortgage interest deduction.
- Property tax deduction.
- Depreciation deduction.
- Capital gains tax deferral (1031 exchange).
- Passive activity loss deduction.
- Deduction for repairs and maintenance.
- Deduction for home office expenses.
- Tax-free cash-out refinance.
- Opportunity zone tax benefits.

CHAPTER 5
THE CAP TRIPOD™

"Real estate investing, even on a very small scale,
remains a tried and true means of building an individual's
cash flow and wealth."

—ROBERT KIYOSAKI, author of Rich Dad Poor Dad

Investing in rental properties involves several key steps—from setting a budget and securing financing to thorough market research and property due diligence before finally completing the purchase of the property. After acquisition, effective property management is also quite important. This includes finding and screening tenants, setting and collecting rent, maintaining the property, and handling tenant relations.

In this chapter, we will explore the entire process of purchasing a rental property from start to finish. I have broken down the process into three fundamental steps, termed the CAP Tripod™, where CAP stands for **Capital**, **Assess**, and **Purchase**. Figure 2 shows the three essential building blocks of the CAP Tripod™ when purchasing a rental investment property.

Figure 2. **CAP Tripod™**

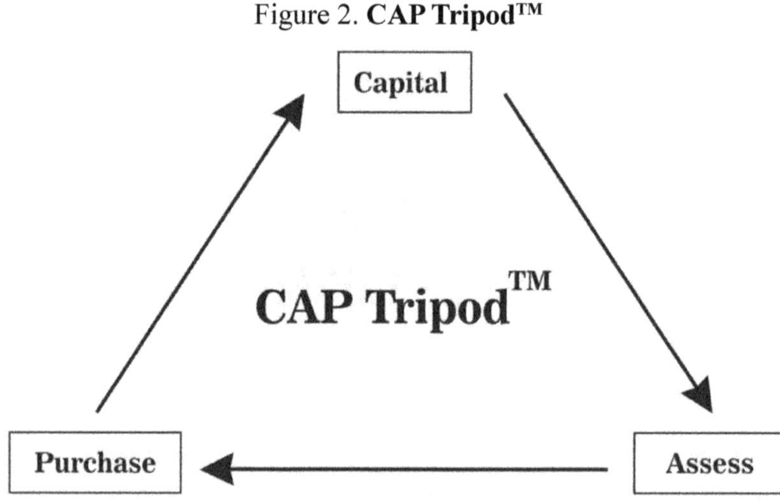

5.1 Capital

In real estate investing, the term 'capital' typically refers to the financial resources or funds that investors use to purchase, maintain, or improve properties. It encompasses both the initial investment required to acquire a property and ongoing expenses related to owning and operating it. When you think about purchasing a rental property, you need to first decide if you will be purchasing the property in cash or financing it. This depends on your individual financial situation, investment goals, and risk tolerance. Both approaches have their advantages and considerations:

If you are able, buying an investment property with cash can have certain advantages like faster closing, no interest payments, and a strong negotiating position. However, there are certain considerations like opportunity cost, tax, and implications that one must keep in mind when purchasing an investment property in cash.

Here are some key advantages and disadvantages of purchasing a rental investment property with cash:

Table 6. **Advantages and Disadvantages of a Cash Purchase**

ADVANTAGES OF A CASH PURCHASE	DISADVANTAGES OF A CASH PURCHASE
Quick Acquisition: Buying a rental property with cash streamlines the purchasing process. There's no need to wait for mortgage approval or deal with potential delays related to financing.	**Opportunity Cost**: Investing a significant amount of cash into a single property means tying up capital that could be used for other investments or emergencies. This limits diversification and may reduce overall portfolio liquidity.
Negotiation Power: Cash buyers often have more negotiation power since they present a guaranteed, hassle-free transaction to sellers. This can lead to opportunities for securing the property at a lower price or with more favorable terms.	**Missed Tax Benefits**: Financing a rental property allows investors to deduct mortgage interest and certain expenses from their taxable income. Cash buyers miss out on these tax deductions, potentially leading to higher tax liabilities.
Increased Cash Flow: With no mortgage payments, cash buyers enjoy higher cash flow from rental income. This increased cash flow can be reinvested into the property for maintenance and improvements or used to expand the investment portfolio.	**Lack of Leverage**: Using cash eliminates the benefits of leverage, which can amplify returns in a rising market. With leverage, investors can control a larger asset base with a smaller initial investment, potentially magnifying gains.
Reduced Risk: Cash purchases eliminate the risk of defaulting on a mortgage and potential foreclosure, providing a sense of security for the investor. Additionally, without mortgage interest payments, there's no exposure to fluctuations in interest rates.	**Reduced Flexibility**: Once cash is invested in a property, it's less liquid compared to other forms of investment. Selling a property to access cash can take time and may incur transaction costs, limiting flexibility in responding to changing market conditions or investment opportunities.
Potential for Higher Returns: By avoiding interest payments, cash buyers may realize higher overall returns on investment compared to financed purchases, especially if the property appreciates in value over time.	**Missed Investment Opportunities**: By committing all available cash to a single property, investors may miss out on other lucrative investment opportunities that arise. This lack of liquidity can hinder the ability to capitalize on market fluctuations or emerging trends.

On the other hand, if you decide to finance the purchase of your rental investment property, there are various avenues to get a loan, such as conventional mortgages, Federal Housing Administration (FHA) loans, Veterans Affairs (VA) loans (if applicable), or portfolio loans from local banks and credit unions. Each option has its own requirements and terms. Most often, you need to first start by saving funds for an initial 'down payment' to the lender. Saving funds requires discipline, planning, and smart financial management. Here are some strategies to help you save funds for a down payment:

- **Set Clear Goals:** Define your financial goals and determine how much money you need to save for the down payment, closing costs, and other expenses associated with purchasing a rental property. Having a specific target will help you stay motivated and focused on your saving efforts.

- **Create a Budget:** Develop a detailed budget that outlines your income, expenses, and savings goals. Track your spending to identify areas where you can cut back or reduce costs and allocate more funds toward your savings goal.

- **Automate Savings:** Set up automatic transfers from your checking account to a dedicated savings account specifically for your rental property fund. Treat your savings like any other recurring expense to ensure consistent contributions over time.

- **Reduce Expenses:** Look for ways to trim unnecessary expenses from your budget, such as dining out less frequently, canceling unused subscriptions or memberships, and finding cheaper alternatives for everyday purchases.

- **Increase Income:** Explore opportunities to increase your income, such as taking on a side job or freelance work, selling unused items, or pursuing higher-paying career opportunities. Allocate any additional income toward your savings goal.

- **Save Windfalls:** Whenever you receive unexpected windfalls, such as tax refunds, bonuses, or cash gifts, resist the temptation to spend them frivolously and instead direct them toward your savings for the rental property.

- **Cut Housing Costs:** Consider downsizing your living arrangements or finding more affordable housing options to free up more money for savings. You could also explore options like renting out a spare room or using platforms like Airbnb to generate extra income from your current residence.

- **Optimize Investments:** If you have existing investments or retirement accounts, review them to ensure they are performing well, and consider reallocating funds to higher-yield investments that can help grow your savings more quickly.

- **Delay Gratification:** Practice delayed gratification by postponing non-essential purchases and focusing on your long-term goal of purchasing a rental property. Remind yourself of the benefits and rewards of achieving financial independence through property investment.

- **Educate Yourself:** Take the time to learn about real estate investing, including different investment strategies, market trends, and financing options. By becoming more knowledgeable about the process, you can make informed decisions that maximize your savings and investment potential.

- **Stay Disciplined:** Stay committed to your savings plan and avoid the temptation to dip into your savings for non-essential expenses. Keep your long-term goals in mind and celebrate milestones along the way to stay motivated.

Once you have saved enough capital to comfortably set aside a 'down payment' for financing, you start to shop around and make a list of various lenders with the best rates and terms that each of them has to offer. The smaller banks and credit unions are a lot easier and more flexible to work with and usually offer competitive financing rates with more favorable terms than some of the bigger banks.

Navigating the landscape of financing options requires a nuanced understanding of the benefits and complexities inherent in leveraging borrowed funds for real estate investment. From the potential for amplified returns through leverage to the tax advantages of mortgage interest deductions, bank loans offer a pathway to maximizing the potential of rental property investments. However, this approach is not without its intricacies and risks, demanding careful assessment and prudent financial management. Here are some key advantages and disadvantages of financing the purchase of a rental investment property:

Table 7. **Advantages and Disadvantages of Financing the Purchase**

ADVANTAGES OF FINANCING THE PURCHASE	DISADVANTAGES OF FINANCING THE PURCHASE
Leverage: Using a bank loan allows investors to leverage their initial investment, meaning they can control a larger asset with a smaller amount of their own money. This amplifies potential returns if the property appreciates in value.	**Interest Costs:** Financing a rental property involves interest payments, which add to the overall cost of the investment. Higher interest rates or longer loan terms can significantly impact cash flow and reduce profitability.
Preservation of Capital: Financing a rental property preserves capital for other investments or emergencies. Investors can use less of their own money upfront, maintaining liquidity and diversification in their investment portfolio.	**Down Payment Requirement:** Banks typically require a down payment of upward of 20% or more for investment properties, which can be a substantial amount of money. This initial cash outlay reduces liquidity and may limit the number of properties an investor can acquire.
Tax Benefits: Mortgage interest and certain expenses related to the rental property are tax-deductible, reducing taxable income and potentially lowering overall tax liabilities. This can result in significant savings for investors.	**Debt Risk:** Taking on debt to finance a rental property carries the risk of default if rental income is insufficient to cover mortgage payments. This risk is heightened during economic downturns or periods of vacancy.
Opportunity for Higher Returns: With leverage, investors have the potential to achieve higher overall returns on investment compared to an all-cash purchase, especially in a rising real estate market.	**Financing Restrictions:** Banks impose certain restrictions and requirements on investment property loans, including minimum credit scores, debt-to-income ratios, and property condition standards. These criteria can limit eligibility and require additional time and effort to secure financing.
Asset Appreciation: As the property appreciates in value over time, the equity in the property increases. This can provide additional borrowing power for future investments or financial flexibility.	**Market Volatility:** Fluctuations in interest rates and property values can impact the affordability and profitability of financed rental properties. Rising interest rates or declining property values may erode cash flow and diminish returns.

There are also many programs available to a first-time home buyer. This includes purchasing your first 'home' with minimal to zero money required for a down payment. Many first-time home buyers who are also aspiring to build wealth through rental properties have bought a two-family or a three-family home with this program. They usually keep one of the units as their primary residence and then rent out the other unit(s) to generate passive income. If you can buy a two-family or a three-family property as your 'primary home,' most often, the rent money from the other units will take care of your monthly mortgage loan payment and leave you with an additional surplus income on the side.

First-time homebuyers have several resources available to help them navigate the process and potentially secure financing. Here are some common resources:

- **Government Programs:** Many governments, federal, state, and local, offer assistance programs for first-time homebuyers, including down payment assistance, grants, and low-interest loans. These programs vary by location, so it is essential to research what is available in your area.

- **HUD Housing Counseling Agencies:** The United States Department of Housing and Urban Development (HUD) provides housing counseling services through approved agencies. These agencies can offer advice on buying a home, navigating the mortgage process, and understanding your rights and responsibilities as a homeowner.

- **Mortgage Programs:** Some lenders offer mortgage programs specifically designed for first-time homebuyers. These programs may have lower down payment requirements or offer more flexible terms.

- **Homebuyer Education Courses:** Many organizations offer homebuyer education courses that cover topics such as budgeting, credit management, and the homebuying process. Completing one of these courses may qualify you for certain assistance programs or help you secure better loan terms.

- **Local Housing Authorities:** Your local housing authority may offer resources and assistance for first-time homebuyers, including information on affordable housing options and programs for low-income buyers.
- **Employer Programs:** Some employers offer homebuyer assistance programs as part of their employee benefits packages. These programs may provide financial assistance or counseling services to help employees purchase their first home.
- **Real Estate Professionals:** Working with a knowledgeable real estate agent or broker can be invaluable for first-time homebuyers. They can help you navigate the market, find properties that meet your needs and budget, and negotiate with sellers on your behalf.
- **Online Resources:** Many online resources are available to help first-time homebuyers, including websites and forums where you can find information and advice from other buyers and experts in the field.

Once you have identified a lender, you request them for a pre-qualification letter. A pre-qualification letter basically states that you, as the borrower, are tentatively approved for a mortgage loan of a certain amount based on your financial information. It is an initial step in the mortgage process and provides an estimate of how much a buyer might be able to borrow. However, it is important to note that a pre-qualification is not a guarantee of a loan; it is simply a preliminary assessment based on the information provided by you, the borrower, to the lender. This letter is often required by real estate agents or sellers to demonstrate a buyer's seriousness and financial capability when making an offer on a property.

A pre-qualification letter is usually based on your down payment amount, your credit history, credit score, liabilities, and other debt. You take the pre-qualification letter from the bank and start your search for an investment property within that amount. Try not to stretch yourself too thin and get tempted to look at properties that exceed the pre-qualified amount.

For investment properties, typically, banks require about a 25% to 30% down payment on the purchase price. There can, however, be some exceptions to this. If you are a first-time homebuyer, some banks allow you to get away with as little as 0% to 5% down. Some lenders even offer a lower down payment if your income level is below a certain threshold, if you have served in the armed forces, or are employed in a certain industry like healthcare or education. When shopping for a loan, it is always helpful to ask lenders if they offer any special incentives for either the down payment, the finance rate, or both.

Ultimately, the decision to buy your first investment rental property with cash or through financing depends on your financial goals, risk tolerance, and investment strategy. It is essential to weigh the advantages and considerations of each approach and choose the option that aligns best with your individual circumstances. Consulting with a financial advisor or real estate professional can help you make an informed decision based on your specific needs and objectives.

5.2 Assess

Once you have raised enough capital and obtained a pre-qualification letter, you begin your search for a rental property. Start off by first making a list of criteria that are important to you in an investment property, such as location, property type (single-family, two-family, commercial, etc.), size, condition, and amenities. Prioritize your criteria based on their importance to your investment goals, but make sure to stay within your financial limits or the pre-approved amount as discussed in the previous section.

After you have identified the location and type of property that you are interested in, explore various sources to review potential investment properties, including online listings, real estate agents, auctions, foreclosure listings, networking with other investors, and off-market opportunities. Be proactive in your search and consider using multiple channels to increase your chances of finding the right property. It is always helpful to engage a reputable and seasoned real estate broker or agent to assist in locating a property suitable for your needs. In many cases, the seller covers the brokerage fee, relieving you of that concern. When exploring properties in various cities or neighborhoods, it is advisable to enlist multiple brokers familiar with the local area or possessing extensive knowledge of the specific neighborhood.

There are some key resources that can help you make informed decisions and minimize risks when looking for a rental property, which have been outlined in chapter 10, titled "Resources." Utilizing these resources can help investors perform comprehensive research, ensuring they make well-informed decisions and mitigate risks when investing in rental properties. It is critical to evaluate and verify all aspects of a property and its potential as an investment prior to making an offer to purchase. This process helps ensure that the investor makes an informed decision, identifies any potential risks or issues, and confirms that the property meets their investment goals.

Some of the essential due diligence factors when looking for a rental investment property include:

1. Location
2. Market trends
3. Property condition
4. Rental Income
5. Operating Expenses
6. Cash Flow
7. Net Operating Income (NOI)
8. Capitalization Rate (CAP)
9. Return on Investment (ROI)
10. Tenant History
11. Rentability
12. Legal Considerations
13. Appreciation Potential
14. Environmental Factors

15. Property Management

16. Risks

17. Exit Strategy

5.2.1 Location:

The adage "location, location, location" still holds true in real estate. A property's location significantly impacts its value, rental income potential, and long-term appreciation. This phrase underscores the idea that the three most important factors influencing the appeal and potential of a property are its location, location, and location.

The location of your investment property can impact the immediate cash flow and the long-term accumulation of equity. For instance, buying a property in a rural area with limited demand for housing or commerce may result in stagnant cash flow and a prolonged wait for appreciation. On the other hand, investing in an area where there is a high demand for housing or commercial space accelerates equity growth and ensures a more consistent monthly cash flow. Here are some important considerations when deciding on the location of your rental property investment:

- **Market Demand:** Research the demand for rental properties in the area. Look for locations with a strong rental market where demand consistently outpaces supply. Factors such as population growth, job opportunities, and migration trends can indicate a healthy rental market.

- **Neighborhood Amenities:** Evaluate the amenities available in the neighborhood, such as schools, parks, shopping centers, restaurants, public transportation, and healthcare facilities. Properties located near desirable amenities tend to attract more tenants and command higher rental rates.

- **Safety and Security:** Safety is a top priority for tenants. Assess the crime rates and overall safety of the neighborhood before investing in a rental property. Choose locations with low crime rates and a reputation for safety to attract quality tenants and reduce vacancy risks.

- **School District:** Consider the quality of the local school district, especially if your target tenant demographic includes families with children. Properties in highly rated school districts tend to appeal to families and may command higher rental rates.

- **Employment Opportunities:** Evaluate the job market and employment opportunities in the area. Properties located near major employment centers or in areas with diverse job opportunities are likely to attract a stable pool of tenants and experience lower vacancy rates.

- **Future Development Plans:** Research any planned or ongoing development projects in the area, such as infrastructure improvements, new commercial developments, or revitalization initiatives. Investing in locations with positive growth prospects can lead to long-term appreciation and increased demand for rental properties.

- **Property Taxes and Regulations:** Understand the property tax rates and regulatory environment in the area. High property taxes or burdensome regulations can impact your cash flow and investment returns. Choose locations with favorable tax policies and landlord-friendly regulations.

- **Rental Income Potential:** Analyze rental market data and comparable rental rates in the area to assess the income potential of your investment property. Calculate potential rental yields and cash flow to ensure the property aligns with your financial goals.

- **Tenant Profile:** Identify your target tenant demographic and choose a location that caters to their needs and preferences. For example, young professionals may prefer urban neighborhoods with access to nightlife and cultural amenities, while families may prioritize suburban areas with good schools and parks.

- **Rental Rates:** Properties in sought-after locations typically command higher rental rates due to increased demand and limited supply.

Investors can capitalize on prime locations by setting competitive rental rates that reflect the value of the neighborhood and amenities available to tenants. Conversely, properties in less desirable locations may struggle to attract tenants or may require lower rental rates to remain competitive.

- **Tenant Demand:** A property located in a desirable area with access to amenities, transportation, employment centers, and reputable schools is more likely to attract a higher volume of potential tenants. Tenants prioritize convenience and quality of life when selecting rental properties, making location a key factor in driving demand.

- **Tenant Retention:** Tenants are more likely to stay longer in rental properties located in desirable neighborhoods with favorable amenities and a high quality of life. Investing in properties with strong location advantages can lead to higher tenant retention rates, reducing vacancy periods and turnover costs for investors.

- **Resilience to Market Fluctuations:** Properties in prime locations tend to be more resilient to market fluctuations and economic downturns. Even during periods of economic uncertainty, rental properties in desirable neighborhoods often maintain their value and rental demand, providing investors with a stable source of rental income and long-term investment growth.

- **Potential for Appreciation:** Location plays a significant role in property appreciation potential. Properties in rapidly growing or up-and-coming neighborhoods are more likely to experience substantial appreciation in value over time, providing investors with opportunities for capital gains and increased equity in their rental properties.

- **Market Stability:** The stability and growth potential of a real estate market depend largely on its location. Some areas experience more consistent appreciation and demand due to factors like economic stability, infrastructure development, and government investment. Investing in stable markets reduces the risk of significant value fluctuations.

- **Risk Management:** Location affects the risk profile of a property investment. Factors such as crime rates, environmental hazards, and susceptibility to natural disasters can vary widely depending on the location. Conducting thorough due diligence on the neighborhood and surrounding area helps investors assess and mitigate potential risks.

- **Resale Potential:** When it comes time to sell an investment property, its location plays a crucial role in determining its resale value and marketability. Properties in desirable locations tend to sell faster and at higher prices than those in less desirable areas.

Investing in a property in a desirable location is often considered a sound long-term investment strategy. Properties in prime locations tend to appreciate in value more rapidly over time compared to those in less favorable areas. Overall, location is a fundamental consideration in real estate investment because it directly impacts property value, rental demand, market stability, risk management, and resale potential. Investors often prioritize properties in prime locations to maximize their returns and mitigate investment risks.

5.2.2 Market Trends:

Market trends refer to the patterns, behaviors, and changes observed in the real estate market over a period of time. These trends can encompass a wide range of factors, including rental prices, vacancy rates, demand for rental properties, housing supply, local economic conditions, population growth or decline, and shifts in tenant preferences. Analyzing market trends is crucial for investors to make informed decisions about purchasing, renting, or managing rental properties. By staying abreast of market trends, investors can identify opportunities, anticipate challenges, adjust their strategies accordingly, and maximize their returns in the rental property market. Some key trends to examine are:

- **Rental Prices:** Market trends encompass fluctuations in rental prices within a given area or neighborhood. Investors monitor changes in rental rates over time to gauge the demand for rental properties and adjust their pricing strategies accordingly. Factors such as supply and demand dynamics, economic conditions, and local market competition can influence rental prices.

- **Vacancy Rates:** Vacancy rates reflect the proportion of rental units that are unoccupied within a specific market. Monitoring vacancy rates helps investors assess the overall health of the rental market and identify potential opportunities or challenges. High vacancy rates may indicate oversupply or declining demand, whereas low vacancy rates suggest a robust rental market with strong tenant demand.

- **Demand for Rental Properties:** Market trends also encompass changes in the demand for rental properties, which can be influenced by factors such as population growth, employment opportunities, migration patterns, and lifestyle preferences. Understanding shifts in tenant demographics and preferences enables investors to target their properties to meet the evolving needs of renters.

- **Housing Supply:** Changes in the supply of rental properties within a market impact rental dynamics and pricing. Investors monitor new construction, housing developments, and inventory levels to assess the level of competition and potential saturation within the rental market. Oversupply can lead to increased vacancies and downward pressure on rental prices, while limited supply may create opportunities for investors to capitalize on high demand.

- **Economic Conditions:** Economic factors such as job growth, income levels, interest rates, and inflation rates play a significant role in shaping market trends in rental property investing. Strong economic indicators typically correlate with increased demand for rental properties and higher rental rates, while economic downturns may result in decreased demand and softer rental markets.

- **Local Market Dynamics:** Market trends are highly localized, meaning that what applies in one market may not necessarily apply in another.

Investors must analyze and understand the specific dynamics of the markets in which they operate, including neighborhood characteristics, local regulations, development plans, and demographic trends.

By monitoring and analyzing market trends in rental property investing, investors can make strategic decisions to optimize their investment portfolios, mitigate risks, and capitalize on emerging opportunities within the dynamic real estate market.

5.2.3 Property Condition:

When evaluating the condition of a property for a rental investment, it is highly recommended to conduct a thorough inspection to assess its overall condition and identify any potential issues that could affect its value, rental income, or require repairs. Here is a checklist of some of the important items to consider:

- **Structural Integrity:** Look for signs of structural damage, including cracks in walls or foundations, sloping floors, or sagging ceilings. Pay attention to the condition of the roof, walls, and foundation.

- **Mechanical Systems:** Inspect the HVAC (heating, ventilation, and air conditioning) system, plumbing, and electrical systems. Check for leaks, outdated wiring, or malfunctioning equipment that may require repair or replacement.

- **Exterior:** Evaluate the condition of the exterior of the property, including the siding, paint, windows, doors, and landscaping. Look for signs of water damage, rot, or pest infestation.

- **Interior:** Assess the condition of the interior spaces, including the walls, ceilings, floors, doors, and windows. Look for signs of water damage, mold, or pest infestation. Check the functionality of doors, windows, and locks.

- **Appliances and Fixtures:** Inspect the condition and functionality of appliances (such as refrigerators, stoves, dishwashers, and washing machines) and fixtures (such as faucets, toilets, and light fixtures). Determine if they need repair or replacement.

- **Safety Features:** Ensure that the property has essential safety features in place, such as smoke detectors, carbon monoxide detectors, fire extinguishers, and proper ventilation. Check that they are in working condition and comply with local building codes and regulations.
- **Accessibility and ADA Compliance:** If applicable, check for accessibility features and compliance with the Americans with Disabilities Act (ADA), such as wheelchair ramps, handrails, and accessible bathrooms.
- **Code Compliance:** Verify that the property meets building codes and zoning regulations. Check for any outstanding permits or violations that may need to be addressed.
- **Environmental Concerns:** Assess any environmental hazards or concerns, such as lead paint, asbestos, radon, or mold. Consider hiring a professional inspector to conduct specialized testing if necessary.
- **Future Maintenance Needs:** Anticipate future maintenance needs and factor them into your budgeting and investment planning. Consider the age and condition of major components, such as the roof, HVAC system, and appliances.
- **Professional Inspection:** Consider hiring a qualified home inspector or contractor to conduct a comprehensive inspection of the property. They can provide expert guidance and identify any hidden issues that may not be apparent during a visual inspection.

By thoroughly evaluating the condition of the property and addressing any concerns upfront, you can make informed decisions and mitigate potential risks when purchasing a rental investment property.

5.2.4 Rental Income:

Income from a rental property typically includes all the revenue generated from renting out the property to tenants.

Here is a breakdown of what is generally considered rental income from an investment property:

- **Rent Payments:** The primary source of income is the rent paid by tenants for the use of the property. This includes regular monthly rent payments as well as any additional rent for services or amenities provided by the landlord.

- **Security Deposits:** Security deposits collected from tenants, which are typically held to cover damages to the property beyond normal wear and tear or unpaid rent.

- **Fees and Charges:** Any fees or charges imposed on tenants, such as late fees, pet fees, parking fees, or fees for amenities like laundry facilities or storage space.

- **Miscellaneous Income:** This may include income from sources such as renting furnishings or equipment (if provided by the landlord), parking, laundry machines, and vending machines on the property, or renting out parts of the property for events or advertising.

Setting a property's rent amount involves evaluating various factors to determine an appropriate sum that balances market demand, property features, and financial considerations. Some of those key factors are:

- **Market Analysis:** Research the local rental market to understand current rental rates for similar properties in the area. Look at online listings, rental advertisements, and property management websites to gather data on rental prices.

- **Comparable Properties:** Look for comparable rental properties in the vicinity to gauge the rental price of the property you're considering. Compare factors such as property type, size, condition, location, and amenities to determine a competitive rental price.

- **Location:** Evaluate the property's location and its impact on rental demand and rental rates. Properties in desirable neighborhoods with good schools, amenities, and proximity to transportation hubs or employment centers generally command higher rents.

- **Property Features and Amenities:** Consider the features and amenities of the property, such as the number of bedrooms, bathrooms, square footage, parking availability, outdoor space, and any special amenities like a pool, gym, or in-unit laundry. Properties with desirable features typically warrant higher rents.
- **Condition of the Property:** Assess the condition of the property and any recent renovations or upgrades that may justify a higher rental price. Well-maintained properties with modern amenities and features often attract higher rents.
- **Tenant Demand:** Consider the demand for rental properties in the area and the quality of tenants you're likely to attract. Properties in high-demand areas with a strong rental market may allow for higher rental prices.
- **Market Trends:** Stay informed about market trends and rental rate fluctuations in the area. Factors such as supply and demand, economic conditions, and seasonal variations can impact rental prices.
- **Tenant Preferences:** Understand the preferences and needs of potential tenants in the area. Tailor the rental price to align with what tenants are willing to pay for similar properties in the market.
- **Utilities and Expenses:** Determine which utilities and expenses (such as property taxes, insurance, maintenance, homeowner's association (HOA) fees, and property management fees) are included in the rent and which are the responsibility of the tenant. Factor in these expenses when setting the rental price.
- **Legal Considerations:** Ensure that the rental price complies with local rent control laws, fair housing regulations, and any other legal requirements governing rental pricing in the area.

By considering these factors and conducting thorough market research, you can determine an appropriate rent amount that maximizes the property's income potential while remaining competitive in the market. Striking a balance between generating rental income and attracting quality tenants is essential to ensuring the long-term success of your rental investment.

5.2.5 Operating Expenses:

Operating expenses of a rental investment property are the ongoing costs associated with owning and maintaining the property. These expenses are subtracted from the rental income to calculate the property's NOI. The most common operating expenses of a rental investment property are:

- **Property Taxes:** Taxes levied by local governments based on the assessed value of the property. Property taxes can vary depending on the location and assessed value of the property.

- **Insurance:** Property insurance covers the property against damages caused by events such as fire, theft, vandalism, and natural disasters. The cost of insurance premiums depends on factors such as the property's location, size, age, and level of coverage.

- **Maintenance and Repairs:** Regular maintenance and repairs are necessary to keep the property in good condition and address wear and tear over time. This includes expenses for routine maintenance tasks like landscaping, cleaning, and painting, as well as repairs to systems and structures.

- **Utilities:** Expenses for utilities such as water, sewer, trash removal, electricity, gas, and heating can be either paid by the landlord or passed on to the tenant through separate utility meters or as part of the rent.

- **Property Management Fees:** If you hire a property management company to handle day-to-day operations, tenant relations, and maintenance tasks, you'll incur management fees, typically calculated as a percentage of the rental income.

- **HOA Fees:** If the property is part of a HOA, you'll need to pay regular HOA fees to cover costs associated with community amenities, maintenance of common areas, and compliance with HOA rules and regulations.

- **Vacancy Losses:** When the property is vacant between tenants, you lose rental income. It's essential to budget for potential vacancy periods and factor in the associated costs such as advertising for new tenants and cleaning between tenancies.

- **Capital Expenditures (CapEx):** These are large expenses for major improvements or replacements of building components, such as a new roof, HVAC system, appliances, or flooring. CapEx expenses are typically less frequent but can be significant when they occur.

- **Property Management Software and Tools:** Expenses related to software, tools, or services used for property management, accounting, tenant screening, and rent collection.

- **Legal and Professional Fees:** Expenses for legal services, eviction proceedings, property inspections, and other professional services related to property ownership and management.

- **Miscellaneous Expenses:** Other miscellaneous expenses such as advertising and marketing costs, property association dues, permits and licenses, and travel expenses related to property management.

By accurately estimating and budgeting for these operating expenses, you can ensure that your rental investment property generates positive cash flow and remains financially viable over the long term. It's essential to monitor expenses regularly and adjust your budget as needed to maintain profitability and maximize returns on your investment.

5.2.6 Cash Flow:

Cash flow in a rental property investment refers to the amount of money generated by the property after subtracting all expenses from the rental income. It represents the net income or profit earned from the property on a periodic basis, typically monthly or annually. Positive cash flow indicates that the rental income exceeds the total expenses, resulting in a surplus of cash, while negative cash flow occurs when the expenses exceed the rental income, resulting in a shortfall of cash.

Here's how cash flow is calculated in a rental property investment:

Cash Flow = Rental Income − (Operating Expenses + Financing Expenses + Taxes + Capital Expenses + Miscellaneous Expenses)

Where:

- **Rental Income:** The total income generated from rent collected from tenants, including any additional sources of rental income like parking, laundry, etc.

- **Operating Expenses:** The ongoing costs associated with owning and maintaining the property, such as property taxes, insurance, maintenance and repairs, utilities, property management fees, HOA fees, vacancy losses, and property management software/tools.

- **Financing Expenses:** Expenses related to financing the property, including interest payments, loan origination fees, points, and other financing costs.

- **Taxes:** Other taxes associated with the property, such as income tax on rental income, local business taxes, and occupancy taxes.

- **Capital Expenses:** Large expenses for major improvements or replacements of building components, such as a new roof, HVAC system, appliances, or flooring. These expenses are less frequent but can have a significant impact on the property's financial performance.

- **Miscellaneous Expenses:** Other miscellaneous expenses such as legal and professional fees, advertising and marketing costs, property association dues, permits and licenses, and travel expenses related to property management.

Positive cash flow indicates that the property is generating surplus income, which can be used to cover operating expenses, finance future investments, pay down debt, or provide ongoing income for the investor. Negative cash flow means that the property is not generating enough income to cover its expenses, requiring the investor to cover the shortfall out of pocket.

Analyzing cash flow is essential for evaluating the financial performance of a rental property, and helps in making informed decisions about the investment in several ways:

- **Profitability Assessment:** Calculating income (rental income, for example) versus expenses (mortgage payments, property taxes, maintenance costs, etc.) allows investors to determine the NOI of the property. The NOI provides a clear picture of how much income the property generates after accounting for all operating expenses. This helps investors assess the profitability of the investment and compare it to alternative investment opportunities.

- **Cash Flow Management:** Positive cash flow, where income exceeds expenses, is essential for covering operating costs, servicing debt, and providing investors with a return on their investment. Monitoring income versus expenses allows investors to manage cash flow effectively, ensuring there are sufficient funds available to cover expenses and potential contingencies.

- **Risk Mitigation:** Understanding the relationship between income and expenses helps investors identify potential risks and vulnerabilities in their investments. For example, if expenses consistently exceed income, it may indicate inefficiencies in property management or unrealistic rental expectations. By addressing these issues, investors can mitigate the risk of financial losses and improve the investment's long-term viability.

- **Investment Planning:** Analyzing income versus expenses enables investors to develop informed investment strategies and make data-driven decisions. For instance, if expenses are projected to increase significantly in the future (e.g., due to rising property taxes or maintenance costs), investors can proactively adjust their financial plans and investment strategies to account for these changes.

- **Leverage and Financing:** Lenders and financial institutions often assess a property's income versus expenses when evaluating loan applications. A healthy income-to-expense ratio demonstrates the property's ability to generate sufficient income to cover expenses and debt service, making it more attractive to lenders and potentially allowing investors to secure more favorable financing terms.

Analyzing the cash flow of a rental property investment is crucial for evaluating its financial viability, assessing its potential ROI, and making informed decisions about property acquisition, management, and financing. It enables investors to optimize returns and ensure the long-term success of their investment endeavors.

5.2.7 Net Operating Income (NOI):

NOI is a key metric used in real estate investment analysis. It represents the income generated from a property after deducting operating expenses, but before deducting any mortgage payments, income taxes, or other non-operating expenses.

In simpler terms, NOI is calculated by taking the total revenue generated by a property (such as rental income, parking fees, and laundry income) and subtracting all the operating expenses necessary to maintain and run the property (such as property taxes, insurance, maintenance costs, property management fees, and utilities). NOI is calculated on an annual basis and represents the property's potential income before accounting for financing or income tax considerations.

NOI = EGI – Operating Expenses

Here is how you calculate the NOI:

- **Gather Income Sources:** Sum up all the income sources generated by the property. This typically includes rental income from tenants, parking fees, laundry income, etc. Exclude any one-time or non-recurring income.

- **Calculate Gross Potential Income (GPI):** This is the total potential income the property could generate if all units were rented at market rates with no vacancies.

  GPI = Rental Income + Other Income

- **Calculate Effective Gross Income (EGI):** Since it's unlikely that all units will be rented at all times, you need to account for vacancy and credit losses. Multiply the GPI by the vacancy rate (expressed as a decimal) to get the EGI.

  EGI = GPI x (1 – Vacancy Rate)

- **Deduct Operating Expenses:** Subtract all operating expenses associated with running the property from the Effective Gross Income. Operating expenses typically include property taxes, insurance, utilities, maintenance, repairs, property management fees, and any other costs directly related to operating the property.

Rental Income + Other Income (parking fees, laundry income) = Gross Potential Income (GPI)

Gross Potential Income (GPI) x (1 – Vacancy Rate) = Effective Gross Income (EGI)

Effective Gross Income (EGI) – Operating Expenses (property taxes, insurance, utilities, maintenance, repairs, and property management fees) = NOI

Once you have calculated the NOI, you can use it to analyze the property's profitability, compare it to similar properties, and make informed investment decisions. NOI also helps calculate the capitalization (CAP) rate for a property which is an important metric for investors because it provides a clear picture of a property's profitability from its core operations. It helps investors evaluate the potential ROI and compare the performance of different properties. Additionally, lenders often use the NOI to determine the maximum loan amount they are willing to provide for a property.

5.2.8 Capitalization Rate (CAP):

Capitalization rate, commonly known as a CAP rate, is a fundamental metric used in real estate investment to evaluate the potential return on a property. It serves as a key indicator of a property's profitability and is essential for investors to assess the viability of an investment opportunity and the associated risk.

CAP rate is a percentage ratio that is calculated by dividing a property's NOI by its current market value or purchase price. The basic formula to calculate a CAP rate is: CAP rate = (Net Operating Income (NOI) / Property Value or Purchase Price) × 100

As an example, let's say you're considering purchasing an apartment building for $1,000,000. You estimate that the annual rental income from the building will be $100,000, and you've calculated the annual operating expenses (property taxes, maintenance, and insurance) to be $30,000.

To calculate the net operating income (NOI), you subtract the annual operating expenses from the annual rental income:

NOI = Rental Income – Operating Expenses

Therefore, NOI = $100,000 – $30,000 = $70,000

Now, to calculate the CAP rate, you divide the NOI by the purchase price:

CAP Rate = (NOI / Purchase Price) x 100

Therefore, CAP Rate = ($70,000 / $1,000,000) x 100 = 7%

So, in this example, the CAP rate for the apartment building is 7%. This means that if you were to purchase the property for $1,000,000, you could expect an annual return of 7% based on the property's net operating income. Keep in mind that CAP rate is just one factor to consider when evaluating a real estate investment, and it should be used in conjunction with other metrics and considerations.

CAP rate is expressed as a percentage and is typically used to assess the rate of return an investor can expect from a real estate investment. CAP rates can vary significantly between markets and property types. For instance, prime commercial properties in major cities might have CAP rates below 5%, indicating lower risk and potentially lower returns, while properties in secondary or tertiary markets might have CAP rates above 10%, suggesting higher risk but potentially higher returns.

There are several ways to interpret a CAP rate:

- **Indicator of Return:** CAP rate gives you an idea of the return you can expect from the property if you were to purchase it outright with cash.

The higher the CAP rate, the higher the potential return, assuming all other factors remain constant.

- **Risk Assessment:** Generally, a higher CAP rate indicates higher risk because it implies a higher potential return but might also signify factors such as lower demand, poorer location, or higher operating costs. Conversely, a lower CAP rate indicates lower risk but potentially lower returns.

- **Comparative Analysis:** CAP rates are useful for comparing different investment opportunities. For example, if you're looking at several properties, comparing their CAP rates can help you decide which one offers the best return relative to its price.

- **Market Conditions:** CAP rates can vary by location and property type. In a competitive market, CAP rates may be lower due to higher demand, driving prices up. Conversely, in a less competitive market or for properties with specific challenges, CAP rates may be higher.

- **Income Stability:** CAP rate assumes a stable income stream. If a property's income is expected to fluctuate significantly, or if there are uncertainties about future income (e.g., expiring leases, high vacancy rates), the CAP rate may not accurately reflect the actual return.

- **Financing Considerations:** While CAP rate provides a snapshot of a property's ROI without considering financing, investors should also factor in financing costs and interest rates to assess the overall profitability of the investment.

While CAP rate is a valuable tool for initial investment analysis, it also has certain limitations:

- **Sensitivity to NOI:** CAP rate is sensitive to changes in NOI, making it crucial for investors to accurately estimate operating expenses and rental income.

- **Market Variability:** CAP rates may vary across different property types, asset classes, and geographic locations, making direct comparisons challenging.

- **Risk vs. Return:** A high CAP rate may indicate attractive returns but could also signify higher risk, requiring thorough due diligence.

In the realm of real estate investing, CAP rate serves as a cornerstone metric for evaluating investment opportunities. By understanding CAP rate and its implications, investors can make informed decisions, mitigate risks, and maximize returns in their investment endeavors. However, it is essential to complement cap rate analysis with comprehensive due diligence and market research to navigate the intricacies of real estate investment successfully.

5.2.9 Return on Investment (ROI):

ROI in real estate investment refers to the measure of profitability and performance of an investment property relative to the amount of capital invested. It is a key metric used by investors to evaluate the efficiency of their investment and to compare different investment opportunities. ROI is typically expressed as a percentage and can be calculated using various formulas, but the basic concept is to determine how much profit an investment property generates relative to its cost.

The formula for calculating ROI in real estate investment is:

ROI = (Net Profit / Total Investment) × 100

Where:

- Net Profit is the income generated from the investment property minus all expenses (including operating expenses, financing costs, property taxes, and maintenance).
- Total Investment represents the total capital invested in acquiring and maintaining the property, including the purchase price, closing costs, renovations, and any other associated expenses.

The ROI provides investors with a clear understanding of the financial performance and efficiency of their investment. A higher ROI indicates a more profitable investment, while a lower ROI suggests lower profitability relative to the investment amount. ROI can be calculated for different time periods (e.g., annually, monthly, or over the entire holding period) and can be adjusted to account for factors such as inflation, taxes, and financing terms.

Investors use ROI to assess the attractiveness of real estate investments, compare different properties or investment opportunities, and make informed decisions about allocating capital. However, it is essential to consider other factors such as risk, market conditions, and investment objectives in addition to ROI when evaluating real estate investments.

5.2.10 Tenant History:

If the property is currently rented, review the payment history of existing tenants, their lease agreements, and any existing tenant issues. It is important to gather comprehensive information about the tenant to assess their past behavior, reliability, and suitability as a renter. Some key items you should check are:

- **Rental Payment History:** Review the tenant's payment history to see if they have consistently paid rent on time. Look for any instances of late payments or missed payments, as this may indicate financial instability or potential issues with rent collection.

- **Lease Compliance:** Assess whether the tenant has complied with lease terms and regulations during their tenancy. This includes adherence to rent payment schedules, property maintenance responsibilities, and compliance with lease agreements and rules.

- **Communication with Landlord:** Evaluate the tenant's communication skills and interaction with you or the previous landlord. Positive communication and cooperative behavior are indicators of a responsible and respectful tenant.

- **Property Condition:** Assess how well the tenant has maintained the property during their tenancy. Look for any signs of damage, neglect, or unauthorized alterations to the property. This includes both the interior and exterior of the rental unit.

- **Lease Renewals and Extensions:** Review the tenant's lease renewal or extension history. A tenant who has consistently renewed their lease may indicate satisfaction with the property and a desire to continue renting.

- **Tenant Complaints or Disputes:** Check if there have been any complaints or disputes involving the tenant during their tenancy. This may include noise complaints, neighbor conflicts, or property damage issues.

- **Eviction History:** Investigate whether the tenant has a history of evictions or legal disputes with previous landlords. Eviction records can indicate potential red flags such as non-payment of rent or lease violations.

- **Legal and Regulatory Compliance:** Ensure that the tenant has complied with all legal and regulatory requirements during their tenancy, including rent control laws, fair housing regulations, and local ordinances.

By conducting a thorough evaluation of the existing tenant's history, you can make informed decisions about lease renewals, tenant retention, and property management strategies. It is essential to balance the tenant's history with other factors such as property condition, market conditions, and investment objectives when assessing their suitability for continued rental.

5.2.11 Rentability:

Several important factors contribute to the rentability of a rental property, which refers to its ability to attract and retain tenants consistently. Here are some key factors that create rentability:

- **Location:** The property's location is one of the most critical factors influencing its rentability. Properties situated in desirable neighborhoods with good schools, amenities, public transportation access, and proximity to employment centers tend to attract more tenants.

- **Property Condition:** The overall condition of the property plays a significant role in its rentability. Well-maintained properties with updated amenities, modern appliances, and clean, attractive interiors are more appealing to prospective tenants.

- **Amenities and Features:** Properties offering desirable amenities such as in-unit laundry facilities, parking spaces, outdoor spaces (e.g., balcony, patio), storage options, and updated kitchens and bathrooms have higher rentability. Features like air conditioning, high-speed internet, and energy-efficient appliances also enhance the property's appeal.

- **Price Competitiveness:** The rental price of the property should be competitive with similar properties in the area. Overpriced rentals may deter potential tenants, while underpriced rentals may raise suspicion or suggest lower quality.

- **Property Management:** Effective property management practices contribute to rentability by ensuring prompt responses to maintenance requests, clear communication with tenants, and proactive efforts to maintain the property's condition and address tenant concerns.

- **Marketing and Advertising:** Effective marketing and advertising strategies help promote the property to potential tenants. Utilizing online rental platforms, social media, signage, and word-of-mouth referrals can attract more tenants and increase rentability.

- **Tenant Screening:** Implementing thorough tenant screening processes helps ensure that qualified and responsible tenants are selected. Screening criteria may include credit checks, rental history verification, employment verification, and criminal background checks.

- **Flexibility in Lease Terms:** Offering flexible lease terms, such as month-to-month leases or short-term leases, can attract tenants seeking temporary housing solutions or flexibility in their living arrangements.

- **Responsive Landlord or Property Manager:** Tenants value landlords or property managers who are responsive, respectful, and attentive to their needs. Being accessible and addressing tenant concerns promptly enhances tenant satisfaction and encourages lease renewals.

- **Safety and Security:** Properties with adequate safety and security measures in place, such as well-lit common areas, secure entry systems, and functioning locks, provide tenants with peace of mind and contribute to rentability.

- **Positive Tenant Experience:** Creating a positive tenant experience by fostering a sense of community, organizing social events or amenities, and maintaining a respectful and welcoming environment can increase tenant satisfaction and retention.

By focusing on the above factors and continuously striving to enhance the property's appeal and tenant experience, landlords and property managers can maximize rentability, attract high-quality tenants, and achieve higher occupancy rates and rental income.

5.2.12 Legal Considerations:

It is essential to consider various legal aspects to ensure compliance with relevant laws and regulations and protect your interests as a potential property owner. Here are some key legal considerations to keep in mind during the property search:

- **Property Zoning and Land Use:** Verify that the property is zoned for residential rental use and complies with local zoning ordinances and land use regulations. Ensure that the intended use of the property aligns with zoning requirements and any applicable restrictions.

- **Property Condition and Disclosures:** Assess the property's condition and inquire about any known defects, hazards, or material disclosures that may affect its value or suitability for rental use. Sellers are typically required to disclose known issues that could affect the property's value or pose risks to occupants.

- **Environmental Assessments:** Conduct environmental assessments, such as soil testing, radon testing, or lead paint inspections, to identify potential environmental hazards or contamination on the property. Address any environmental concerns and ensure compliance with environmental regulations.

- **Title and Ownership:** Verify the property's ownership and review the title history to ensure that the title is clear of any liens, encumbrances, or legal disputes. Obtain a title insurance policy to protect against potential title defects or claims.

- **Property Taxes and Assessments:** Research the property's tax history, including property tax assessments, unpaid taxes, and any special assessments or tax liens. Understand your tax obligations as a property owner and budget for property taxes accordingly.

- **Legal Restrictions and Covenants:** Review any legal restrictions, covenants, conditions, and easements that may affect the property's use, development, or resale. Understand the implications of restrictive covenants or HOA rules on rental operations and tenant rights.

- **Tenant Rights and Rent Control:** Familiarize yourself with federal, state, and local landlord-tenant laws governing rental housing, including tenant rights, eviction procedures, fair housing practices, security deposits, rent control, and habitability standards. Ensure compliance with applicable tenant protection laws.

- **Insurance Coverage:** Consider insurance coverage for the property, including property insurance, liability insurance, and landlord insurance (e.g., renter's insurance). Understand the types of insurance coverage available and assess the risks associated with property ownership and rental operations.

- **Market Regulations and Trends:** Stay informed about market regulations, trends, and economic factors that may impact rental property investments. Research local market conditions, vacancy rates, rental demand, and potential changes in rental laws or regulations that could affect property values or rental income.

- **Legal Assistance:** Seek legal advice from qualified real estate attorneys or legal professionals to review contracts, purchase agreements, and legal documents related to the property purchase. Obtain professional guidance on legal matters and address any legal questions or concerns before proceeding with the property acquisition.

By considering these legal considerations during the property search process, investors can mitigate risks, ensure legal compliance, and make informed decisions when selecting a rental investment property. Consulting with legal professionals and conducting thorough due diligence can help protect your interests and maximize the success of your rental property investment.

5.2.13 Appreciation Potential:

When looking for a rental investment property, it is important to consider the appreciation potential, which refers to the property's ability to increase in value over time. Here are several factors to keep in mind when assessing appreciation potential:

- **Location:** The property's location is a primary driver of appreciation potential. Properties located in desirable neighborhoods with strong economic growth, good schools, amenities, and proximity to employment centers tend to appreciate faster than properties in less desirable areas.

- **Economic Indicators:** Evaluate local economic indicators such as job growth, population growth, income levels, and unemployment rates. Strong economic fundamentals contribute to housing demand and drive property appreciation in the long term.

- **Development and Infrastructure:** Consider planned or ongoing development projects, infrastructure improvements, and urban revitalization efforts in the area. Investments in transportation, public utilities, and community amenities can enhance property values and stimulate economic growth.

- **Housing Market Trends:** Monitor housing market trends such as supply and demand dynamics, inventory levels, median home prices, and sales trends. A balanced or limited housing supply coupled with strong demand can lead to price appreciation in the local housing market.

- **Historical Performance:** Review historical property appreciation trends in the area to assess the property's past performance and potential for future appreciation. Analyze historical sales data, price trends, and market conditions to identify patterns and forecast future appreciation.

- **Property Features and Upgrades:** Consider the property's features, condition, and potential for value-added improvements. Properties with desirable amenities, modern upgrades, and well-maintained conditions are more likely to appreciate in value over time.

- **Neighborhood Development:** Evaluate the neighborhood's development trajectory and potential for gentrification or revitalization. Investments in infrastructure, commercial development, and public amenities can drive property appreciation and attract higher-income residents.

- **School District Quality:** Research the quality of local school districts and their impact on property values. Properties located in highly rated school districts tend to command higher prices and experience greater appreciation due to demand from families seeking quality education.

- **Market Demand Drivers:** Identify key demand drivers for rental properties in the area, such as population growth, demographic trends, lifestyle preferences, and housing preferences. Tailor your investment strategy to meet the needs of target tenant demographics and capitalize on market demand drivers.

- **Rental Market Conditions:** Assess rental market conditions, vacancy rates, rental demand, and rental income potential in the area. Strong rental market fundamentals and positive rental income prospects can support property appreciation by attracting investors and stabilizing property values.

By considering these appreciation potential factors when evaluating rental investment properties, investors can make informed decisions, maximize long-term returns, and build wealth through real estate investment. It's important to conduct thorough market research, due diligence, and financial analysis to assess appreciation potential and mitigate investment risks.

5.2.14 Environmental Factors:

When purchasing a rental investment property, it is important to consider environmental factors that could impact the property's value, appeal, and potential risks. Here are some key environmental factors to keep in mind:

- **Location:** The property's location can be influenced by various environmental factors, such as proximity to natural amenities (e.g., parks, lakes), environmental hazards (e.g., flood zones, seismic activity), and pollution sources (e.g., industrial sites, highways). Choose a location with favorable environmental conditions and minimal risks.

- **Natural Hazards:** Assess the property's exposure to natural hazards such as floods, earthquakes, hurricanes, wildfires, and landslides. Properties located in high-risk areas may require additional insurance coverage or mitigation measures to reduce potential damage and liability.

- **Environmental Contamination:** Investigate the presence of environmental contaminants such as asbestos, lead-based paint, mold, radon, and soil contamination (e.g., from previous industrial or agricultural activities). Conduct environmental assessments and inspections to identify potential hazards and ensure compliance with environmental regulations.

- **Air Quality:** Consider the air quality in the property's vicinity, including pollution levels, allergens, and industrial emissions. Poor air quality can affect tenant health and well-being, as well as property value and marketability.

- **Water Quality:** Evaluate the quality of drinking water sources, including municipal water supplies and private wells. Test for contaminants such as lead, bacteria, pesticides, and chemicals to ensure the safety of the water supply for tenants and comply with regulatory standards.

- **Waste Management:** Investigate waste management practices in the area, including garbage disposal, recycling programs, and hazardous waste management. Ensure that the property has appropriate waste collection and disposal facilities to maintain cleanliness and compliance with local regulations.

- **Environmental Regulations:** Stay informed about environmental regulations and zoning laws that may impact property development, construction, and land use. Ensure compliance with environmental permits, restrictions, and mitigation requirements imposed by regulatory agencies.

- **Sustainability and Energy Efficiency:** Consider incorporating sustainable and energy-efficient features into the property to reduce environmental impact, lower utility costs, and attract environmentally conscious tenants. This may include energy-efficient appliances, LED lighting, solar panels, low-flow fixtures, and green building materials.

- **Ecological Impact:** Assess the property's impact on local ecosystems, habitats, and wildlife. Avoid disturbing sensitive habitats or protected species and incorporate landscaping practices that promote biodiversity and conservation.

- **Climate Change Resilience:** Anticipate the potential effects of climate change, such as rising sea levels, extreme weather events, and temperature fluctuations. Invest in resilient building designs, infrastructure upgrades, and disaster preparedness measures to mitigate risks and ensure the property's long-term viability.

Environmental risks can significantly impact the value of the property and the cost of property insurance coverage. Properties located in flood zones, areas prone to soil contamination, or regions with a history of natural disasters may be perceived as higher risk by potential buyers, leading to decreased demand and lower property values. Insurance companies also assess the level of risk associated with a property based on factors such as its location, susceptibility to environmental hazards, and potential for damage from natural disasters. Properties located in high-risk areas may face higher insurance premiums or difficulty obtaining coverage.

By considering these environmental factors during the property search and acquisition process, investors can make informed decisions, mitigate risks, and create sustainable and resilient rental investments that benefit both tenants and the environment.

5.2.15 Property Management:

Owing an investment property and making it a lucrative asset requires good management. You can either manage the property on your own or hire a professional management company.

Managing a property starts with vetting good tenants. The last thing you want is to have a difficult tenant who does not respect the property or fails to pay their rent on time. This could drastically affect the cash flow of the investment, turning it from an asset into a liability.

Once you have a good tenant, you want to make sure that it becomes a mutually synergistic relationship. The tenant respects the premises and pays their rent on time, and you, as the landlord, maintain the property and show the tenants that you care for their comfort and safety. As the landlord, this means being available to help the tenant if they call with a property-related issue that may arise at any given time.

Most people buy investment properties as a side hustle from their 'main employment' to help generate a source of passive income. It can become difficult for some landlords to take time out from work or family to check on a tenant or the property on a regular basis. This is where management companies come in and take over the entire operation of running a property, from vetting tenants to collecting rent to answering phone calls and taking care of any maintenance or repair work needed at the property.

Some Management Companies and/or Property Managers charge a flat fee, while others charge upward of 4% of the rent collected to manage a property. Some companies are known to even charge as high as 10% of the gross rents collected. If you are just starting out and have a single-family or two-family home, it might be more economical to manage the property yourself and save on the management fee. However, if you are buying a multi-family property or have several properties, then it might make sense to hire a professional property manager.

When looking to hire a management company or a property manager, do your due diligence and look for someone with enough experience in the field. Also, look up their reviews online—not just from other property owners but also from the tenants they manage. It is important to ask a range of questions to ensure they are competent, trustworthy, and a good fit for your needs.

Here are some key questions to ask when looking for a management company or a property manager:

1. Experience and Qualifications:
- How long have you been managing rental properties?
- How many properties do you currently manage?
- Do you have any specific certifications or licenses related to property management?
- Can you provide references from current or past clients?

2. Services Provided:
- What services are included in your management fee?

- How do you handle maintenance and repair issues?
- What is your process for tenant screening?
- How do you handle tenant disputes and evictions?
- Do you offer regular property inspections? How often are they conducted?
- What is your policy on handling emergencies?

3. Fees and Costs:

- What is your management fee structure?
- Are there any additional fees for services such as leasing, renewals, or inspections?
- How do you handle maintenance and repair costs? Do you markup vendor invoices?
- What is your process for collecting rent and handling late payments?

4. Marketing and Leasing:

- How do you market vacant properties?
- What is your average vacancy rate for the properties you manage?
- How do you set rental rates for properties?
- What is your average time to lease a vacant property?

5. Communication and Reporting:

- How do you communicate with property owners?
- How often will I receive updates and reports about my property?
- Can I access my property information online?

6. Legal and Compliance:

- Are you familiar with local, state, and federal landlord-tenant laws?
- How do you ensure compliance with fair housing regulations?
- Do you have experience handling legal issues related to rental properties?

7. Contract and Termination:

- What is the term of your management contract?

- What is the process for terminating the contract if I am not satisfied with your services?
- Are there any penalties or fees for early termination of the contract?

8. Miscellaneous:

- How do you handle tenant turnover and make-readies?
- What technology or software do you use to manage properties?
- Do you invest in rental properties yourself? If so, how do you manage them?

These questions will help you gauge the property manager's experience, reliability, and approach to managing rental properties, ensuring you select the best candidate for your investment. To successfully manage a rental property, a property manager must have a comprehensive understanding of various aspects of property management and execute a wide range of tasks efficiently.

Here is a detailed breakdown of what a property manager needs to know and do:

Knowledge Areas:

1. Real Estate Laws and Regulations:

- Familiarize with federal, state, and local housing laws.
- Understand tenant rights and landlord responsibilities.
- Know fair housing laws to avoid discrimination.

2. Financial Management:

- Learn how to set and adjust rental rates.
- Understand budgeting, accounting, and financial reporting.
- Know tax implications and benefits related to rental properties.

3. Property Maintenance:

- Basic knowledge of property maintenance and repairs.
- Understand preventive maintenance schedules and emergency repair protocols.

4. Marketing and Leasing:

- Effective marketing strategies for attracting tenants.

- Knowledge of different advertising platforms and techniques.
- Lease agreement terms and conditions.

5. *Tenant Relations:*
- Effective communication and conflict resolution skills.
- Screening and background check processes.

6. *Technology and Tools:*
- Use of property management software for tasks like rent collection, maintenance requests, and tenant communication.

Key Tasks:

1. *Marketing and Advertising:*
- Create compelling property listings with detailed descriptions and quality photos.
- Advertise on various platforms including online listings, social media, and local classifieds.

2. *Tenant Screening and Selection:*
- Conduct thorough background checks including credit, rental history, and criminal records.
- Evaluate applications fairly and select qualified tenants.

3. *Lease Management:*
- Draft and manage lease agreements.
- Ensure all lease terms comply with legal requirements.
- Collect security deposits and handle lease renewals.

4. *Rent Collection and Financial Management:*
- Set up efficient systems for rent collection.
- Enforce rent payment policies and handle late payments.
- Maintain accurate financial records and prepare reports.

5. *Property Maintenance and Repairs:*
- Schedule regular inspections and routine maintenance.
- Respond promptly to repair requests.
- Coordinate with contractors and service providers for major repairs.

6. Handling Tenant Issues and Complaints:
- Address tenant complaints and resolve issues professionally.
- Enforce lease terms and handle violations appropriately.

7. Legal Compliance and Risk Management:
- Ensure compliance with all relevant housing laws.
- Keep up-to-date with changes in regulations.
- Manage risk through proper insurance coverage and safety protocols.

8. Record Keeping and Documentation:
- Maintain detailed records of all transactions, communications, and property-related documents.
- Ensure confidentiality and security of tenant information.

9. Communication and Customer Service:
- Maintain open lines of communication with tenants.
- Provide excellent customer service to foster positive tenant relationships.

10. Continuing Education and Professional Development:
- Stay updated on industry trends and best practices.
- Attend relevant training sessions, workshops, and industry conferences.

Practical Steps to Implement:

1. Develop a Comprehensive Management Plan:
- Outline your management strategies, including marketing, tenant selection, and maintenance plans.

2. Utilize Technology:
- Invest in property management software to streamline operations and improve efficiency.

3. Build a Reliable Network:
- Establish connections with contractors, real estate agents, and legal advisors.

4. Create Clear Policies and Procedures:

- Develop and enforce policies for tenant screening, rent collection, maintenance, and lease violations.

5. Ensure Legal and Regulatory Compliance:

- Regularly review and update practices to align with current laws and regulations.

By mastering these knowledge areas and executing these tasks effectively, a property manager can ensure the successful management of rental properties, providing a positive experience for both landlords and tenants. Once you and the management company or the property manager agree on the terms, it is highly recommended that you draft an agreement that both parties must sign. This way, both you and the property manager would have clear and defined expectations of each other. It is probably in your best interest to have your attorney review the agreement before it is fully executed.

5.2.16 Risks:

When buying a rental property, it is essential to consider various risks that could affect your investment. Here are some common risks associated with rental properties:

- **Vacancy Risk:** The property may experience periods of vacancy, resulting in a loss of rental income. Factors such as economic conditions, market saturation, or tenant turnover can contribute to vacancy risk.

- **Tenant Risk:** Problematic tenants can pose risks such as late or missed rent payments, property damage, or legal disputes. Conduct thorough tenant screening processes to mitigate this risk, including background checks, credit checks, and rental history verification.

- **Market Risk:** Fluctuations in the real estate market, such as changes in property values, rental demand, or interest rates, can impact the investment's profitability. Economic downturns or oversupply in the rental market can increase market risk.

- **Maintenance and Repair Risk:** Rental properties require ongoing maintenance and repairs to keep them in good condition. Unexpected repairs, such as plumbing issues or roof leaks, can incur significant costs and affect cash flow.

- **Regulatory and Legal Risk:** Landlord-tenant laws and regulations vary by jurisdiction and can affect your rights and obligations as a property owner. Non-compliance with regulations, such as fair housing laws or building codes, can lead to fines, legal disputes, or even eviction delays.

- **Property Damage and Insurance Risk:** Damage to the property from natural disasters, accidents, or vandalism can result in repair costs and loss of rental income. Adequate insurance coverage, including property insurance and liability insurance, can help mitigate this risk.

- **Financing and Interest Rate Risk:** If you finance the purchase of the rental property with a mortgage or loan, changes in interest rates can affect your monthly mortgage payments and overall investment returns. Rising interest rates can increase borrowing costs and reduce cash flow.

- **Taxation and Regulatory Changes:** Changes in tax laws, such as deductions for rental property expenses or property tax rates, can impact your investment's profitability. Stay informed about tax regulations and consult with tax professionals to understand the tax implications of your investment.

- **Economic and Geopolitical Risks:** Economic factors such as inflation, unemployment, or geopolitical events can impact the rental market and property values. Diversifying your investment portfolio and staying informed about macroeconomic trends can help mitigate these risks.

- **Liquidity Risk:** Real estate investments are relatively illiquid compared to other investment assets. Selling a rental property may take time and incur transaction costs, especially during market downturns or if the property has limited appeal to potential buyers.

Here are a few case studies with real-life examples detailing the background, strategy, outcome, and lesson learned to help mitigate common risks associated with rental property investing:

Case Study 1: MANAGING TENANT RISK

» **Background:** Jane Smith invested in a duplex property in a growing suburban area. She aimed to generate steady rental income to supplement her retirement. However, Jane faced significant tenant-related issues early on, including late payments, property damage, and eventual eviction proceedings.

» **Strategy:** To mitigate tenant risks, Jane implemented the following strategies:

1. **Screening Process:** Jane enhanced her tenant screening process by conducting thorough background checks, including credit history, employment verification, and rental history.

2. **Lease Agreement:** She revised her lease agreement to include clear terms regarding rent payment, property maintenance, and penalties for late payments.

3. **Security Deposit:** Jane increased the security deposit requirement to cover potential damages and unpaid rent.

4. **Property Management:** Jane hired a professional property management company to handle tenant relations, maintenance requests, and rent collection.

» **Outcome:** After implementing these strategies, Jane saw a significant improvement in tenant quality and reliability. The property management company efficiently handled tenant issues, reducing Jane's stress and involvement. Rent payments became timely, and property maintenance improved, leading to higher tenant satisfaction and retention.

» *Lesson Learned:* Proper tenant screening and professional property management can significantly mitigate risks related to tenant behavior, leading to more stable and predictable rental income.

Case Study 2: HANDLING MAINTENANCE AND REPAIR COSTS

» *Background:* John and Mary invested in a small apartment building in an older neighborhood. While the location was promising, the building required frequent repairs, leading to unexpected expenses and impacting their cash flow.

» *Strategy:* To manage maintenance and repair costs, John and Mary implemented the following strategies:

1. **Preventive Maintenance:** They developed a preventive maintenance schedule to address minor issues before they became major problems. Regular inspections and upkeep reduced the likelihood of expensive repairs.

2. **Reserve Fund:** They established a reserve fund specifically for maintenance and repairs, setting aside a portion of rental income each month.

3. **Vendor Relationships:** They built relationships with reliable contractors and service providers, negotiating better rates for regular work.

4. **Insurance:** They reviewed and upgraded their property insurance to ensure adequate coverage for potential damages and repairs.

» *Outcome:* By proactively managing maintenance and repairs, John and Mary were able to control costs and avoid major financial surprises. The reserve fund provided a safety net, and strong vendor relationships ensured timely and cost-effective repairs. Their property remained in good condition, attracting quality tenants and maintaining its value.

» *Lesson Learned:* Proactive maintenance planning and financial preparedness are crucial for managing and mitigating maintenance and repair costs, ensuring the long-term viability of the investment.

Case Study 3: NAVIGATING MARKET RISKS

» ***Background:*** Alex invested in a rental property in a city experiencing rapid growth. Initially, rental demand was high, and Alex enjoyed strong rental income. However, an economic downturn led to increased vacancy rates and downward pressure on rental prices.

» ***Strategy:*** To navigate market risks, Alex employed the following strategies:

1. **Diversification:** Alex diversified his investment portfolio by purchasing properties in different locations and markets. This spread the risk and reduced reliance on a single market.

2. **Flexible Leasing:** He offered flexible leasing terms, including short-term leases, to attract a broader range of tenants during periods of high vacancy.

3. **Market Analysis:** Alex continuously monitored market trends and economic indicators to make informed decisions about rental pricing and property improvements.

4. **Marketing Efforts:** He increased marketing efforts, using online platforms and local advertising to reach potential tenants.

» ***Outcome:*** Alex's diversified portfolio helped stabilize his overall rental income despite fluctuations in individual markets. The flexible leasing terms and enhanced marketing efforts attracted new tenants, reducing vacancy rates. Continuous market analysis enabled Alex to adjust his strategy promptly in response to changing conditions.

» ***Lesson Learned:*** Diversification, flexibility, and market awareness are key to mitigating market risks in rental property investing. Being proactive and adaptable allows investors to navigate economic fluctuations and maintain stable income.

Case Study 4: ADDRESSING LEGAL AND REGULATORY RISKS

» **Background:** Emily purchased a multi-family rental property in a city with stringent rental regulations. She faced challenges in understanding and complying with various legal requirements, leading to fines and legal disputes with tenants.

» **Strategy:** To address legal and regulatory risks, Emily adopted the following strategies:

1. **Legal Consultation:** She consulted with a real estate attorney to understand local rental laws and regulations thoroughly.

2. **Compliance Checklist:** Emily created a compliance checklist to ensure adherence to all legal requirements, including safety standards, tenant rights, and property inspections.

3. **Lease Updates:** She regularly updated lease agreements to reflect current laws and regulations, ensuring clarity and legality.

4. **Education:** Emily educated herself about landlord-tenant laws and attended local real estate workshops and seminars.

» **Outcome:** By taking a proactive approach to legal compliance, Emily avoided further fines and legal issues. Clear and updated lease agreements minimized disputes, and regular legal consultations kept her informed about any regulatory changes. Her property operated smoothly within the legal framework, providing a secure investment.

» **Lesson Learned:** Staying informed and compliant with local laws and regulations is essential for rental property investors. Legal consultation and continuous education help mitigate legal and regulatory risks, ensuring a smooth and lawful operation.

These case studies illustrate the importance of proactive risk management strategies in rental property investing. By addressing tenant risks, maintenance costs, market fluctuations, and legal compliance, investors can enhance the stability and profitability of their rental properties. Conducting thorough due diligence, maintaining adequate reserves, and implementing risk management measures can help protect your investment and maximize returns over the long term.

5.2.17 Exit Strategy:

Exit strategy refers to the plan or approach that an investor intends to use to sell or dispose of a rental investment property at some point in the future if needed. It is essentially a roadmap outlining how an investor intends to exit or liquidate their investment to achieve their financial goals. Here are some common strategies that investors use:

- **Hold and Rent:** This is one of the most common exit strategies for rental investment properties. The investor purchases the property with the intention of holding it for an extended period and renting it out to generate rental income. The property is held as a long-term investment, with the potential for ongoing cash flow, property appreciation, and equity buildup over time.

- **Fix and Flip:** Some investors purchase rental investment properties with the intention of renovating or improving them to increase their value and then selling them for a profit in a relatively short period. This strategy, known as "fix and flip," involves purchasing properties below market value, making strategic renovations or upgrades, and then selling them at a higher price to realize capital gains.

- **Cash-out Refinance:** A cash-out refinance is a financial strategy used by property owners to tap into the equity of a property by refinancing the existing mortgage with a new one that has a higher principal balance. In a cash-out refinance, the property owner borrows more than the remaining balance on the current mortgage, allowing them to receive a lump sum of cash from the equity built up in the property. The property owner can use the cash for various purposes, such as funding renovations, paying off high-interest debt, investing in additional properties, or covering personal expenses. The new mortgage obtained through the cash-out refinance will have updated terms, including a new interest rate, loan term, and monthly payment amount. It's essential for property owners to consider the impact of these changes on their overall financial situation and rental property cash flow.

- **Sell for Cash Flow:** In some cases, investors may decide to sell a rental investment property to unlock equity or realize capital gains. This could be motivated by changes in market conditions, investment goals, or personal circumstances. The proceeds from the sale can be reinvested in other properties or used for other financial purposes.

- **1031 Exchange:** A 1031 exchange, also known as a like-kind exchange, allows investors to defer capital gains taxes by exchanging one rental investment property for another of equal or greater value. This strategy allows investors to leverage their equity and upgrade to properties with potentially higher returns without triggering immediate tax liabilities.

- **Legacy Planning:** Some investors may purchase rental investment properties with the intention of holding them as part of a long-term wealth-building and legacy planning strategy. The properties are held as assets that can be passed down to heirs or beneficiaries as part of an estate plan, providing ongoing income and wealth for future generations.

- **Diversification:** Investors may choose to exit a rental investment property to diversify their real estate portfolio or allocate capital to other investment opportunities. By selling underperforming properties or rebalancing their portfolio, investors can optimize their asset allocation and mitigate investment risk.

The choice of an exit strategy for a rental investment property depends on factors such as investment objectives, market conditions, property performance, financial considerations, and personal goals. It's essential for investors to carefully evaluate their options and develop a strategic exit plan that aligns with their long-term financial goals and risk tolerance.

5.3 Purchase

Once you have been pre-approved for a loan, and identified a potential investment property that meets your criteria, the next step is to make an offer and negotiate the purchase price and terms with the seller. After the price and terms are agreed upon, you conduct due diligence and finally close on the property.

The entire process, from making an offer to the purchase of the property, involves several steps:

1. Making an Offer:

- Determine your offer price based on market comparables, property condition, rental potential, and your investment goals.
- Draft a purchase offer, including the proposed purchase price, earnest money deposit, contingencies (such as inspection and financing), and desired closing timeline.
- Submit the offer to the seller or their listing agent, either directly or through your real estate agent.
- The seller may accept your offer, reject it, or counter with a different price or terms.
- Negotiate with the seller to reach mutually acceptable terms that satisfy both parties' interests for an "accepted offer."

2. Purchase and Sale Agreement (P&S):

- Once both parties agree on the terms and conditions of the sale, they sign a P&S agreement, whereby the property is considered "under contract" or "under agreement."
- During this period, earnest money is typically deposited into an escrow account to show the buyer's commitment to the transaction.

3. Due Diligence:

- Conduct inspections, property appraisals, and any additional due diligence to assess the property's condition and verify information provided by the seller.
- Review financial lease agreements, tenant records (if applicable), property income/expense reports, zoning regulations, tax returns, and any other pertinent documents.
- Finalize your financing arrangements, property insurance, title insurance, etc.
- Address any issues uncovered during inspections or due diligence, such as repair negotiations or resolution of title issues.
- Waive contingencies once satisfied or negotiate further if needed.

4. Pre-Closing:

- Coordinate with your escrow or closing agent to schedule the closing date and time.
- Review the closing disclosure statement and ensure all financial details are accurate.

5. Closing:

- Attend the closing meeting to sign the necessary documents, including the purchase agreement, loan documents (if applicable), and other closing paperwork.
- Pay closing costs, which may include loan origination fees, title insurance, escrow fees, and property taxes.
- Receive the keys to the property and officially take ownership.

6. Post-Closing:

- Transfer utilities and insurance coverage to your name.
- Communicate with tenants (if any) about the change in ownership and provide necessary contact information.
- Implement your management plan for the rental property, including any repairs or improvements planned.

5.3.1 Making an Offer:

Making an offer to purchase an investment rental property involves several steps to ensure that you present a strong and competitive offer. Here's a general guide to the process:

- **Research the Market:** Begin by researching the local real estate market to understand property values, rental rates, and demand in the area. This information will help you determine a fair market value for the property you're interested in.

- **Review Property Listings:** Look for investment rental properties that meet your criteria, such as location, size, price range, and potential rental income. Work with a real estate agent or use online listing platforms to find suitable properties.

- **Conduct Due Diligence:** Before making an offer, conduct thorough due diligence on the property. This includes reviewing property disclosures, inspecting the property for any issues or repairs needed, and researching the property's history, such as past rental income and expenses.

- **Determine Your Offer Price:** Based on your research and due diligence, determine the offer price you're willing to submit for the property. Consider factors such as the property's condition, comparable sales in the area, potential rental income, and your investment goals.

- **Calculate Your Financing:** Determine how you will finance the purchase of the property, whether through cash, a conventional mortgage, or another type of financing. Get pre-approved for a mortgage if you plan to finance the purchase.

- **Prepare Your Offer:** Work with your real estate agent to prepare a written offer to purchase the property. Include details such as the offer price, proposed closing date, earnest money deposit amount, contingencies (such as financing and inspection contingencies), and any other terms or conditions you wish to include.

- **Submit Your Offer:** Once your offer is prepared, submit it to the seller or the seller's agent. Your real estate agent can help you submit the offer and negotiate with the seller on your behalf.
- **Negotiate Terms:** Be prepared to negotiate with the seller if they counter your offer or if there are multiple offers on the property. Work with your real estate agent to negotiate the best possible terms for your purchase.
- **Finalize Purchase Agreement:** Once your offer is accepted, work with your real estate agent and attorney to finalize the Purchase and Sale Agreement (P&S).

5.3.2 Purchase and Sale Agreement (P&S):

A Purchase and Sale Agreement, also known as a Sales Contract or Purchase Agreement, is a legally binding contract between a buyer and a seller outlining the terms and conditions of a real estate transaction. This document serves as a roadmap for the sale of a property and typically includes the following key elements:

- **Identification of Parties:** The agreement identifies the buyer(s) and seller(s) involved in the transaction, including their legal names and contact information.
- **Property Description:** A detailed description of the property being sold, including its address, legal description, and any relevant parcel identification numbers.
- **Purchase Price:** The agreed-upon purchase price for the property, as well as the currency in which the payment will be made. The purchase price may also include details about the deposit or earnest money paid by the buyer to secure the transaction.
- **Contingencies:** Any conditions or contingencies that must be met for the sale to proceed, such as obtaining financing, satisfactory home inspections, or the sale of the buyer's current property.

- **Financing Details:** If the purchase is contingent on the buyer obtaining financing, the agreement may specify the type of loan, the lender, and any deadlines for securing financing.
- **Closing Date:** The date on which the closing of the sale will take place, at which point the ownership of the property will transfer from the seller to the buyer.
- **Closing Costs:** A breakdown of the closing costs associated with the transaction, including fees for title insurance, attorney fees, transfer taxes, and other expenses.
- **Property Condition:** Any representations or warranties made by the seller regarding the condition of the property, as well as any disclosures of known defects or issues.
- **Seller's Obligations:** The seller's responsibilities leading up to the closing, such as maintaining the property in its current condition and providing access for inspections and appraisals.
- **Buyer's Obligations:** The buyer's responsibilities leading up to the closing, such as securing financing, completing inspections, and obtaining insurance.
- **Earnest Money Deposit:** The amount of money paid by the buyer as a good faith deposit to demonstrate their commitment to the transaction. This deposit is typically held in escrow until the closing of the sale.

Once both parties have agreed to the terms outlined in the Purchase and Sale Agreement, and the document has been signed by both the buyer and seller, it becomes a legally binding contract. Failure to adhere to the terms of the agreement can result in legal consequences for the party in breach of the contract.

5.3.3 Due Diligence:

Conducting thorough due diligence prior to closing is essential to assess the property's financial viability, potential risks, and overall suitability for investment. This includes a comprehensive property inspection, a detailed review of the property's financial documents, completing a professional appraisal of the property, and obtaining property insurance and title insurance.

PROPERTY INSPECTION:

Conducting a thorough home inspection is a critical step to assess the property's condition and identify any potential issues or maintenance needs. The first step is to hire a qualified and experienced home inspector. It's essential to choose an inspector who is licensed or certified and has a good reputation for thoroughness and attention to detail. Once the home inspector is selected, schedule the inspection at a mutually convenient time with the seller or their representative. It is typically recommended to attend the inspection so you can ask questions and discuss any concerns directly with the inspector.

During the inspection, the home inspector will thoroughly evaluate the property's structural components, exterior features, roof, plumbing, electrical systems, heating and cooling systems, appliances (if included), and other interior components. They will look for signs of damage, deterioration, safety hazards, and code violations. A thorough home inspection can give you valuable insights into the condition of the rental investment property and make informed decisions to protect your investment. When conducting a property inspection, there are several key areas you should pay close attention to:

- **Structural Integrity:** Check for any signs of structural damage, such as cracks in the walls, uneven floors, or sagging ceilings. Look for water damage, especially around windows, doors, and in the basement.
- **Roof:** Inspect the roof for missing or damaged shingles, signs of leaks, and the overall condition of the gutters and downspouts.

- **Plumbing:** Check for leaks under sinks, around toilets, and in the basement or crawl space. Test water pressure and ensure all faucets and drains are working properly.

- **Electrical System:** Look for outdated wiring and overloaded circuits, and check that all outlets and light switches are functioning correctly. Inspect the electrical panel for any signs of damage or wear.

- **HVAC System:** Test the heating and cooling systems to ensure they are working efficiently. Check the age of the furnace and air conditioner, and inquire about their maintenance history.

- **Appliances:** If the property comes with appliances, such as a refrigerator, stove, dishwasher, or washer/dryer, test each one to ensure they are in working condition.

- **Windows and Doors:** Check for drafts around windows and doors, and ensure they open and close properly. Inspect the condition of the window frames and screens.

- **Insulation and Ventilation:** Assess the insulation in the attic and walls to ensure adequate energy efficiency. Check ventilation systems in bathrooms, kitchens, and the attic to prevent moisture buildup.

- **Pests:** Look for signs of pest infestation, such as droppings, gnaw marks, or nests. Common pests include rodents, insects, and termites.

- **Exterior:** Inspect the exterior of the property, including the siding, foundation, and landscaping. Look for any signs of damage or deterioration, such as cracks, rot, or water stains.

- **Safety Features:** Verify the presence of smoke detectors, carbon monoxide detectors, and fire extinguishers. Check that all safety features are in working order.

- **Documentation:** Request any relevant documentation, such as permits, warranties, or inspection reports, to ensure everything is up to code and properly maintained.

After the inspection is complete, the inspector will provide a detailed inspection report outlining their findings and recommendations. Review the report carefully to understand the property's condition and any issues that may need attention. If the inspection reveals significant issues or concerns, you may have the option to negotiate with the seller to address repairs or provide credits to offset the cost of repairs. Your real estate agent can help facilitate these negotiations and advise you on the best course of action.

Armed with the information from the inspection report, you can make informed decisions about whether to move forward with the purchase, renegotiate the terms of the sale, or potentially walk away from the deal if the inspection reveals serious issues that cannot be resolved satisfactorily. Even if the inspection doesn't uncover any major issues, it's important to recognize that all properties require ongoing maintenance and upkeep. Use the information from the inspection report to create a maintenance plan for the property to help protect your investment and ensure the long-term profitability of your rental investment.

FINANCIAL DOCUMENTS:

When purchasing a rental investment property, reviewing various financial documents is essential to assess the property's financial performance, potential risks, and overall investment value.

Here is a comprehensive list of financial documents that you should review:

1. Income Statements (Profit and Loss Statements):

- Review the property's income statements to analyze its revenue and expenses over a specific period.
- Income statements provide valuable insight into the property's rental income, operating expenses, and NOI.

2. Rent Rolls:

- Examine the property's rent rolls, which list details of each tenant's lease agreement, including rental rates, lease terms, and payment history.

- Rent rolls help assess the property's current occupancy status, rental income, and potential for future income growth.

3. Lease Agreements:

- Review existing lease agreements between the landlord and tenants to understand the terms and conditions of the rental agreements.
- Lease agreements provide information about rental rates, lease terms, security deposits, and tenant responsibilities.

4. Tax Returns:

- Request copies of the property owner's tax returns, including Schedule E (Supplemental Income and Loss), which reports rental income and expenses.
- Tax returns provide a comprehensive overview of the property's financial performance and tax implications for the owner.

5. Utility Bills:

- Review utility bills for the property, including electricity, gas, water, sewer, and trash disposal.
- Utility bills help assess the property's operating expenses and identify any patterns or fluctuations in utility costs.

6. Property Insurance Policies:

- Obtain copies of the property's insurance policies, including hazard insurance, liability insurance, and any additional coverage such as flood insurance or earthquake insurance.
- Review insurance policies to understand the property's coverage, deductibles, premiums, and potential risks.

7. Property Tax Assessments:

- Obtain copies of recent property tax assessments and tax bills for the property.
- Property tax assessments provide information about the property's assessed value, tax rate, and annual property taxes.

8. Operating Expense Records:

- Review records of the property's operating expenses, including maintenance and repair costs, property management fees, landscaping expenses, and other recurring expenses.
- Operating expense records help assess the property's ongoing expenses and budget for future maintenance and repairs.

9. Capital Expenditure History:

- Examine records of past capital expenditures for the property, such as major renovations, upgrades, or repairs.
- Capital expenditure history provides insight into the property's maintenance needs and potential future investment requirements.

10. Financial Projections and Budgets:

- Review financial projections and budgets prepared by the property owner or property management company.
- Financial projections help assess the property's potential for rental income growth, expense management, and overall investment returns.

By thoroughly reviewing these financial documents, you can gain a comprehensive understanding of the rental investment property's financial performance, potential risks, and overall investment value. This information is essential for making informed decisions and maximizing the property's investment potential.

PROPERTY APPRAISAL:

A property appraisal is an evaluation of a property's value conducted by a qualified appraiser to determine its market worth. It provides an objective assessment of a property's market value, which is essential for making informed investment decisions. Accurate appraisals help investors determine a fair purchase price, ensuring they do not overpay and can achieve a profitable ROI.

Appraisals also play a key role in securing financing, as lenders require them to gauge the property's worth and associated risk. Moreover, understanding the property's value aids in setting appropriate rental rates, attracting tenants, and maintaining competitive pricing within the local market. Additionally, appraisals can identify potential issues or needed repairs, enabling investors to budget accordingly and avoid unexpected expenses. Overall, a thorough appraisal is a foundational step that supports financial planning, risk management, and strategic decision-making in rental property investing.

A property appraisal serves several purposes:

- **Determining Market Value:** The primary purpose of a property appraisal is to establish the current market value of the rental investment property. The appraiser considers factors such as the property's location, size, condition, features, and comparable sales in the area to determine its fair market value.

- **Validating Purchase Price:** A property appraisal helps validate the purchase price of the rental investment property. By comparing the appraised value to the agreed-upon purchase price, buyers can ensure that they are paying a fair price for the property based on its market value.

- **Securing Financing:** Lenders often require a property appraisal as part of the mortgage approval process for financing a rental investment property. The lender wants assurance that the property's value supports the loan amount being requested by the buyer. The appraisal helps mitigate the risk for the lender by ensuring that the property serves as adequate collateral for the loan.

- **Negotiation Tool:** In some cases, the results of a property appraisal can be used as a negotiation tool during the purchase process. If the appraised value is lower than the agreed-upon purchase price, buyers may use the appraisal to negotiate a lower purchase price with the seller or request concessions to bridge the gap.

- **Investment Analysis:** For investors, a property appraisal provides valuable insight into the potential ROI and overall investment viability. By understanding the property's appraised value relative to the purchase price and projected rental income, investors can assess the property's investment potential and make informed decisions.

Conducting a thorough property appraisal involves several key steps to ensure an accurate assessment of its value and potential profitability. The process begins with pre-appraisal preparation, where all relevant documents, such as property deeds, prior appraisals, recent sales data, and rental income statements, are collected. This is followed by a physical inspection of the property, where the appraiser examines both the exterior and interior, noting the condition, size, layout, and any necessary repairs or maintenance issues. Next, the comparable sales analysis (comps) is conducted, where the appraiser identifies recently sold properties similar in size, condition, location, and amenities to establish a market value benchmark. The income approach is then applied, assessing the property's potential rental income by analyzing current and projected rental rates, occupancy levels, and operating expenses, calculating the NOI, and applying a capitalization rate. Additionally, the cost approach is used to estimate the cost of replacing the property with a similar one, factoring in current construction costs and depreciation, which is particularly useful for new or unique properties. Analyzing market trends is also crucial, as it involves evaluating the current real estate market conditions, economic factors, and local zoning regulations to predict future property values and rental income potential.

Once all these steps are completed, the appraiser synthesizes the findings to arrive at a final valuation, reflecting the property's current market conditions and income potential. This information is compiled into a detailed appraisal report, which includes all methodologies and the final valuation. Finally, the report is reviewed and verified for accuracy before being presented to relevant stakeholders, such as investors and lenders, to inform investment decisions, secure financing, and set rental rates.

Overall, a property appraisal is a critical step when purchasing a rental investment property. It helps buyers and lenders make informed decisions based on the property's true market value, thereby reducing the risk of overpaying or encountering financing challenges down the line.

PROPERTY INSURANCE:

Obtaining property insurance for a rental investment property involves several steps to ensure that the property is adequately protected against a broad range of risks that could lead to significant financial loss. Property Insurance usually covers damages caused by natural disasters, such as fires, storms, or floods, ensuring that the investor is not left with the burden of costly repairs or even total loss. It also safeguards against vandalism and theft, which can be common concerns for rental properties. Furthermore, property insurance typically includes liability coverage, protecting the investor from legal claims if a tenant or visitor is injured on the premises. This coverage extends to legal fees and medical expenses, shielding the investor from substantial out-of-pocket costs. By providing a safety net for unexpected events and liabilities, property insurance helps maintain the investment's profitability and stability. It also enhances the property's attractiveness to potential tenants, who often look for well-maintained and secure living environments. Overall, property insurance is a critical tool for risk management in rental property investing, ensuring the long-term protection and financial health of the investment.

Begin by researching different insurance providers and policies to find one that meets your needs and budget. Consider factors such as coverage options, deductibles, premiums, and customer reviews. You can obtain quotes from multiple insurance companies to compare prices and coverage. Determine the type and level of coverage you need for your rental investment property. Standard landlord insurance typically includes coverage for the physical structure of the property, liability protection, and loss of rental income coverage.

Depending on the location and specific risks associated with the property, you may also need additional coverage for hazards such as floods, earthquakes, or hurricanes. Once you've identified potential insurance providers, contact them to discuss your insurance needs and obtain quotes. Provide detailed information about the rental property, including its location, size, age, construction materials, and any safety features or upgrades. Carefully review the policy options provided by each insurance company, paying attention to coverage limits, exclusions, deductibles, and any additional endorsements or riders available. Make sure the policy aligns with your coverage needs and provides adequate protection for your rental investment property.

There are several key factors to keep in mind to ensure you get adequate coverage:

- **Type of Coverage:** Understand the types of coverage available, including dwelling coverage (for the physical structure), personal property coverage (for items within the property), liability coverage (to protect against lawsuits), and loss of rental income coverage (to compensate for lost income if the property becomes uninhabitable).

- **Coverage Limits:** Make sure the coverage limits are sufficient to cover the replacement cost of the property and any potential liabilities. Consider factors such as the property's value, location, and local building costs.

- **Deductibles:** Understand the deductible amount you'll be responsible for in the event of a claim. A higher deductible typically results in lower premiums but means you'll pay more out of pocket before insurance kicks in.

- **Exclusions and Limitations:** Review the policy carefully to understand what is covered and what is excluded. Some common exclusions include floods, earthquakes, and certain types of damage caused by neglect or lack of maintenance.

- **Additional Coverage Options:** Consider additional coverage options based on your specific needs, such as flood insurance, earthquake insurance, umbrella liability insurance, or coverage for specific risks like vandalism or loss of rental income.

- **Insurance Company Reputation:** Research the reputation and financial stability of the insurance company. Look for reviews and ratings from independent agencies like A.M. Best, Moody's, or Standard & Poor's.

- **Discounts and Savings:** Inquire about any discounts or savings you may qualify for, such as multi-policy discounts, discounts for safety features like smoke detectors or security systems, or discounts for landlords who have multiple properties insured with the same company.

- **Policy Terms and Conditions:** Understand the terms and conditions of the policy, including any requirements for regular inspections or maintenance, as well as the process for filing claims and any limitations on coverage.

- **Local Regulations:** Be aware of any local regulations or requirements related to property insurance for rental properties in your area, such as minimum coverage requirements or specific types of coverage mandated by law.

- **Review and Update Regularly:** Periodically review your insurance coverage to ensure it remains adequate for your needs. Factors such as changes in property value, renovations or improvements, or changes in local building codes may necessitate adjustments to your coverage.

After selecting a policy, complete the application process by providing the necessary information and documentation requested by the insurance company. This may include details about the property, your ownership status, rental income, and any previous insurance claims. Once you've submitted the application, the insurance company will review the information provided and assess the risk associated with insuring the rental property. This process, known as underwriting, may involve verifying property details, conducting inspections, and assessing your insurance history.

Once the underwriting process is complete and the policy is approved, you'll receive confirmation of coverage. After the policy is approved, review the terms and conditions carefully to ensure they align with your expectations. Once you're satisfied with the policy terms, you can purchase the insurance policy by paying the required premiums. Keep track of your insurance policy's expiration date and be prepared to renew it annually or as required. Stay in touch with your insurance provider to update coverage as needed, especially if there are changes to the property or rental arrangements.

TITLE INSURANCE:

Purchasing title insurance for a rental investment is an important step in protecting your ownership rights and financial interests in the property. It provides protection against potential legal disputes and financial losses related to the property's title. When acquiring a rental property, investors must ensure that the title is clear of any liens, encumbrances, or ownership disputes that could jeopardize their investment. Title insurance offers a safety net by thoroughly examining public records and identifying any issues that could affect the property's ownership status. If any undiscovered defects arise after the purchase, such as forgery, fraud, or undisclosed heirs, title insurance covers the legal expenses and potential losses associated with resolving these claims. This protection not only secures the investor's financial interests but also facilitates smooth transactions, as lenders often require title insurance to mitigate their risks. Additionally, having title insurance enhances the marketability of the property, providing future buyers with confidence in the property's clear title status. In essence, title insurance is an essential component of risk management in rental property investing, ensuring peace of mind and financial stability for investors.

Here is a general guide on how to purchase title insurance:

- **Select a Title Insurance Company:** Research and choose a reputable title insurance company to provide coverage for your rental investment property. Look for companies with experience in the local real estate market and positive reviews from clients.
- **Work with a Title Insurance Agent or Attorney:** Contact a title insurance agent or real estate attorney to assist you with the purchase

of title insurance. They can guide you through the process and help ensure that your interests are protected.

- **Order a Title Search:** The title insurance company will conduct a title search on the property to uncover any existing liens, encumbrances, or defects in the title that could affect your ownership rights. The title search helps identify any potential issues that need to be addressed before closing.

- **Review the Title Commitment:** Once the title search is completed, the title insurance company will provide a title commitment or preliminary title report. Review the title commitment carefully to verify the property's legal description, ownership history, and any title defects that need to be addressed.

- **Address Title Issues:** If the title commitment reveals any title defects, such as unpaid liens or unresolved legal claims, work with your title insurance agent or attorney to resolve these issues before closing on the property. This may involve clearing title defects, obtaining lien releases, or negotiating with creditors.

- **Purchase Title Insurance Policy:** Once any title issues are resolved, you can proceed to purchase a title insurance policy. The title insurance company will provide you with a policy that protects your ownership rights and financial interests in the property against covered risks, such as title defects, fraud, or forgery.

- **Closing Process:** At the closing, you will sign the necessary documents to finalize the purchase of the property and obtain title insurance. The title insurance company will issue the title insurance policy and collect the premium for coverage.

- **Payment of Premium:** Pay the title insurance premium, which is a one-time fee based on the property's purchase price or loan amount. The premium is typically paid at closing and covers the cost of title insurance coverage for as long as you own the property.

- **Retention of Title Insurance Policy:** Keep a copy of the title insurance policy for your records. The title insurance policy provides protection against covered risks for as long as you own the property and can be used to file a claim if any title issues arise in the future.

By following these steps, you can purchase title insurance for your rental investment property and protect your ownership rights and financial interests against potential title defects or claims. Working with experienced professionals, such as title insurance agents or real estate attorneys, can help ensure a smooth and successful transaction.

5.3.4 Pre-Closing:

Before closing on your rental property, there are several important factors to keep in mind to ensure a smooth and successful transaction:

- **Review Closing Documents:** Carefully review all closing documents provided by your real estate agent or attorney. These documents may include the purchase agreement, settlement statement, loan documents (if applicable), and any other paperwork related to the sale.
- **Ensure Financing Is in Place:** If you're obtaining financing for the purchase, double-check that your mortgage loan is approved and that all necessary paperwork has been submitted to the lender. Confirm the details of your loan, including the interest rate, terms, and closing costs.
- **Perform a Final Walk-Through:** Conduct a final walk-through of the property to ensure that everything is in order and that any agreed-upon repairs or improvements have been completed satisfactorily. Verify that all included items are present and in the expected condition.
- **Arrange for Insurance:** Arrange for property insurance to be in place before closing. This includes both hazard insurance to protect against damage to the property and liability insurance to protect against lawsuits.

- **Transfer Utilities:** Arrange for the transfer of utilities into your name effective as of the closing date. This ensures that you have uninterrupted access to essential services such as water, gas, electricity, and internet.

- **Coordinate with Professionals:** Coordinate with your real estate agent, attorney, lender, and any other professionals involved in the transaction to ensure that all necessary tasks are completed on time. Address any questions or concerns you may have with them before closing.

- **Prepare Funds for Closing Costs:** Prepare the necessary funds to cover closing costs, which may include lender fees, title insurance, appraisal fees, property taxes, and prepaid expenses such as homeowners insurance and escrow reserves.

- **Review Closing Disclosure:** Review the closing disclosure provided by the lender at least three days before closing. Verify that all terms of the loan are accurate and that there are no unexpected fees or charges.

- **Obtain Title Insurance:** Purchase title insurance to protect against any issues with the title of the property, such as liens or encumbrances. Review the title commitment and address any concerns with the title company.

- **Plan for Moving:** If you or your tenants will be moving into the property after closing, make sure to plan accordingly. Arrange for moving services, transfer or setup of utilities, and any other necessary preparations for the move.

By keeping these considerations in mind and staying organized throughout the closing process, you can ensure a smooth and successful closing for your rental property purchase.

5.3.5 Closing:

A closing, also known as settlement or escrow, is the final step in the process of transferring ownership of a property from the seller to the buyer. It is the culmination of all the negotiations, inspections, and paperwork involved in a real estate transaction. On the agreed-upon closing date, the buyer and seller, along with their respective agents and possibly other parties such as attorneys and lenders, meet to sign the closing documents. The buyer pays the remaining funds due, including closing costs and down payment, and the seller transfers ownership of the property to the buyer.

Here is what typically happens during a real estate closing:

- **Preparation of Documents:** Prior to the closing date, various legal documents are prepared by the parties involved, including the purchase agreement, mortgage documents (if applicable), and any other required paperwork.

- **Review of Documents:** On the closing day, the buyer and seller, along with their respective real estate agents and attorneys (if any), gather to review and sign the necessary documents. These documents may include the deed, bill of sale, loan documents, title insurance policies, and closing statements.

- **Payment of Funds:** The buyer brings funds to cover the down payment, closing costs, and any other expenses associated with the transaction. These funds are typically provided in the form of a cashier's check or wire transfer.

- **Transfer of Ownership:** Once all documents are signed and funds are exchanged, the title to the property is transferred from the seller to the buyer. This usually involves the recording of the deed with the appropriate government office to officially document the change of ownership.

- **Distribution of Funds:** Any proceeds from the sale, after deducting expenses such as mortgage payoff, real estate commissions, and closing costs, are distributed to the seller. Similarly, any funds required to pay off existing liens or mortgages on the property are disbursed.

- **Closing Statement:** At the end of the closing, the parties receive a closing statement, also known as a settlement statement or HUD-1 form, which outlines all the financial transactions related to the sale.

Once the closing process is complete, the buyer takes possession of the property, and the seller vacates the premises. The closing is a significant milestone in a real estate transaction, after which the deed and other documents are recorded with the appropriate government office, marking the official transfer of ownership to the buyer and the completion of the sale.

5.3.6 Post-Closing:

After closing on the rental property, there are several important tasks you will need to take to ensure a smooth transition and successful management of the property. Here is a checklist of things to consider:

- **Review the Lease Agreements:** If there are existing tenants in the property, review the lease agreements to familiarize yourself with the terms and conditions of the tenancy.

- **Notify Tenants of Change in Ownership:** Inform the tenants in writing about the change in ownership and provide them with your contact information for future communication.

- **Collect Rent and Security Deposits:** If applicable, collect rent and any security deposits from tenants according to the terms of their lease agreements.

- **Transfer Utilities:** Transfer responsibility for utilities such as water, electricity, gas, and trash collection into your name or set up new accounts if necessary. Ensure that tenants are aware of any changes in utility billing.

- **Insurance Coverage:** Obtain landlord insurance or update your existing policy to ensure adequate coverage for the rental property.

Landlord insurance typically provides liability protection and coverage for property damage.

- **Establish Financial Records:** Set up a system for tracking income and expenses related to the rental property. This may include opening a separate bank account for rental income and expenses and keeping detailed records of all transactions.

- **Schedule Property Inspections:** Conduct a thorough inspection of the rental property to assess its condition and identify any maintenance or repair needs. Schedule regular inspections to ensure the property remains in good condition.

- **Address Maintenance and Repairs:** Address any maintenance or repair issues identified during the inspection or reported by tenants. Promptly respond to maintenance requests to maintain tenant satisfaction and preserve the value of the property.

- **Familiarize Yourself with Landlord-Tenant Laws:** Familiarize yourself with federal, state, and local landlord-tenant laws and regulations that govern rental properties in your area. Ensure compliance with all legal requirements, including property maintenance standards, rent control ordinances, and eviction procedures.

- **Establish Communication Channels:** Maintain open and effective communication channels with tenants to address their concerns, provide timely updates, and ensure a positive landlord-tenant relationship.

- **Market Vacancies:** If there are vacant units in the property, develop a marketing strategy to attract new tenants. Advertise vacancies through online listings, signage, and other relevant channels to reach potential renters.

By completing these tasks after closing on a rental property, you can effectively manage the property, maintain positive relationships with tenants, and maximize the return on your investment.

Here are some case studies detailing successes and failures in rental property investing:

Case Study 1: SUCCESS

- » **Background:** John is an investor who decided to purchase a rental property in a growing neighborhood in a metropolitan area. He thoroughly researched the local real estate market, considering factors like job growth, population trends, and rental demand. After finding a promising property within his budget, he purchased it with a mortgage and started renting it out.

- » **Strategy:** John focused on maintaining the property well and providing excellent tenant service. He promptly addressed any maintenance issues and ensured the property was always in good condition. He also screened potential tenants rigorously to find reliable renters who would pay on time and take care of the property.

- » **Outcome:** Over time, John's rental property became highly profitable. The rental income consistently exceeded his mortgage payments and other expenses, allowing him to build equity in the property. As property values in the neighborhood appreciated, John's investment grew even more valuable. Eventually, he was able to refinance the property and use the equity to purchase additional rental properties, further expanding his portfolio.

- » **Lesson Learned:** John's success demonstrates the importance of thorough research, proactive property management, and selecting the right tenants. By investing in a promising location and maintaining a high standard for his rental property, he was able to generate significant long-term returns.

Case Study 2: FAILURE

» ***Background:*** Sarah invested in a rental property in a tourist-heavy area near the beach. She was attracted to the property's potential for high rental income during the peak season. However, she underestimated the off-season demand and overestimated the property's rental potential.

» ***Strategy:*** Sarah invested heavily in renovating the property to attract high-paying vacationers during the summer months. She also priced the rental rates at a premium to maximize her returns during the peak season.

» ***Outcome:*** While Sarah's rental property performed well during the summer months, generating substantial income, it struggled to attract renters during the off-season. The property remained vacant for extended periods, leading to significant losses. Additionally, the high maintenance costs associated with the property, such as landscaping and pool maintenance, further eroded her profits. Unable to cover her expenses during the off-season, Sarah eventually had to sell the property at a loss.

» ***Lesson Learned:*** Sarah's failure highlights the importance of considering seasonality and rental demand fluctuations when investing in vacation rental properties. Overreliance on peak-season income without a sustainable strategy for off-peak periods can lead to financial difficulties. It's crucial to conduct thorough market research and financial analysis before investing in vacation rentals, taking into account both the potential rewards and risks.

Case Study 3: SUCCESS

» ***Background:*** Christina, a young professional, decided to purchase a two-family home in a suburban neighborhood. She was attracted to the idea of living in one unit while renting out the other as a source of passive income. After careful consideration, Christina found a property that met her criteria and financial goals.

» **Strategy:** Christina's strategy was to use the rental income from the second unit to help offset her mortgage payments and other expenses associated with homeownership. She chose to live in one unit herself, allowing her to closely monitor the property and address any maintenance issues promptly. Christina also conducted a thorough screening of potential tenants for the second unit to ensure reliable rental income and minimize the risk of problematic tenants.

» **Outcome:** By living in one unit and renting out the other, Christina was able to significantly reduce her housing expenses. The rental income from the second unit covered a substantial portion of her mortgage payments, property taxes, and insurance costs. This allowed her to save more money for future investments and other financial goals. Additionally, Christina enjoyed the benefits of homeownership, such as building equity in the property and having control over her living space.

» **Lesson Learned:** Christina's experience demonstrates the potential benefits of purchasing a two-family home for owner occupancy and rental income. By strategically leveraging rental income to offset housing expenses, she achieved greater financial stability and accelerated her journey toward long-term wealth building. However, Christina's success also underscores the importance of careful tenant selection and proactive property management to mitigate risks and maximize returns in real estate investing.

Case Study 4: FAILURE

» **Background:** Mark, an inexperienced investor, was drawn to the idea of passive income through rental property investing. He purchased a single-family home in a suburban area without conducting thorough market research or financial analysis.

» **Strategy:** Mark assumed that rental income would easily cover his mortgage payments and expenses, allowing him to profit from the property without much effort. However, he neglected to consider factors such as property maintenance, vacancy rates, and unexpected expenses.

» **Outcome:** After purchasing the property, Mark encountered several challenges. He struggled to find reliable tenants, leading to frequent vacancies and periods of negative cash flow. Additionally, he underestimated the costs of property maintenance and repairs, which ate into his profits. Unable to sustain the financial burden, Mark eventually sold the property at a loss, realizing that he had underestimated the complexities of rental property investing.

» **Lesson Learned:** Mark's failure highlights the importance of conducting thorough due diligence and financial analysis before investing in rental properties. Neglecting key factors such as market demand, property management, and financial projections can lead to costly mistakes. It's essential for investors to educate themselves about the intricacies of real estate investing and seek guidance from experienced professionals to mitigate risks and maximize potential returns.

CAP Tripod™ with key steps involved when purchasing a rental investment property:

CAPITAL

- Review personal finances and savings.
- Save funds for a down payment (if necessary).
- Explore financing options such as mortgages, loans, or partnerships for purchasing the rental property and obtain a pre-approval letter from the lender.

ASSESS

- Conduct thorough market analysis to identify promising locations and property types based on investment goals.

- Evaluate properties based on criteria such as location, condition, potential for appreciation, and rental income potential.
- Inspect the property for any structural issues or maintenance needs.
- Review financial records, including rental income, expenses, and taxes.
- Verify zoning regulations, property taxes, and insurance requirements.

PURCHASE

- Negotiate purchase price and terms with the seller.
- Secure financing through a mortgage lender or other financing options.
- Complete due diligence, property appraisal, property inspection.
- Close the deal by signing the necessary legal documents and transferring funds.
- Prepare the property for rental by completing any necessary repairs or renovations.
- Screen tenants thoroughly by conducting background checks, credit checks, and rental history verification.
- Collect rent payments and manage ongoing maintenance and repairs.
- Regularly review financial performance and monitor rental income and expenses.

CHAPTER 6

INCORPORATING A RENTAL PROPERTY

"Real estate cannot be lost or stolen, nor can it be carried away. Purchased with common sense, paid for in full, and managed with reasonable care, it is about the safest investment in the world."

—FRANKLIN D. ROOSEVELT, former President of the United States

Once you purchase a rental investment, you might want to consider putting the property in an incorporation. Incorporating a rental investment property refers to structuring the ownership of the property within a legal entity, such as a corporation or limited liability company. This process separates the ownership of the property from individual ownership and creates a distinct legal entity to hold and manage the investment. By incorporating a rental investment property, investors gain certain advantages such as limited liability protection, potential tax benefits, and enhanced credibility. It also allows for easier management and transfer of ownership interests. Some common ways to incorporate a rental investment property are:

- **Sole Proprietorship:** This is the simplest form of ownership where you own and manage the property yourself. It offers full control but also exposes you to personal liability.

- **Partnership:** You can co-own the property with one or more partners, sharing the responsibilities, costs, and profits. Partnerships can be general (equal sharing) or limited (one partner has more control or liability protection).

- **Limited Liability Company (LLC):** Forming an LLC separates your personal assets from those of the rental property, providing liability protection. LLCs are popular for rental properties because they offer some of the benefits of both corporations and partnerships.

- **Corporation:** Creating a corporation (such as an S Corporation or C Corporation) can offer liability protection and potential tax advantages. However, it involves more formalities, such as filing additional forms and double taxation, and may have higher administrative costs compared to other structures.

- **REIT:** If you want to invest in rental properties without directly owning them, you can invest in REITs. REITs pool investors' money to purchase and manage income-generating real estate properties. They offer the benefits of diversification and professional management.

- **Tenancy in Common (TIC):** In a TIC arrangement, multiple individuals own separate interests in the property. Each owner can sell, transfer, or mortgage their share independently. TICs are common for larger commercial properties.

- **Trust Ownership:** You can place the property in a trust, which offers certain tax benefits and estate planning advantages. Trust ownership allows you to specify how the property will be managed and distributed to beneficiaries.

Some key steps when incorporating a real estate investment are:

- **Choose a Suitable Legal Structure:** Decide on the type of legal entity you want to create for your real estate investment. Common options include Limited Liability Company (LLC), corporation, Real Estate Investment Trust (REIT), Limited Partnership (LP), General Partnership (GP), or Sole Proprietorship.

- **Select a Unique Name:** Choose a distinct name for your entity and ensure it's not already in use by checking with the appropriate state authority.

- **Draft and File Articles of Incorporation or Organization:** Prepare and submit the necessary formation documents to the state where you intend to incorporate. Articles of Incorporation for corporations or Articles of Organization for LLCs are examples.

- **Obtain an Employer Identification Number (EIN):** Apply for an EIN from the IRS. This unique number is used to identify your business entity for tax purposes.

- **Create Operating Agreement or Bylaws:** For LLCs, an operating agreement outlining ownership, management, and operation details is essential. Corporations need bylaws to establish how the company will be governed.

- **Open a Business Bank Account:** Set up a separate bank account in the name of the entity to manage finances related to real estate investments. This separation of personal and business finances is crucial for liability protection and accurate record keeping.

- **Register for Necessary Business Licenses or Permits:** Depending on your location and the nature of your real estate investments, you may need to obtain specific licenses or permits from local, state, or federal authorities.

- **Transfer Funds or Assets:** Capitalize the entity by transferring funds or assets into its name. These resources will be used for acquiring and managing real estate properties.

- **Develop an Investment Strategy:** Define your investment goals, risk tolerance, target markets, and property types. This strategy will guide your real estate investment decisions.

- **Conduct Due Diligence:** Thoroughly evaluate potential real estate investments by analyzing their financial performance, conducting property inspections, and researching market conditions.

- **Negotiate Purchase Agreements and Financing Terms:** Negotiate favorable terms for acquiring properties and securing financing if necessary. This may involve negotiating purchase prices, loan terms, and other transaction details.

- **Close on Real Estate Transactions:** Once agreements are reached, finalize the purchase transactions by signing closing documents and transferring ownership of the properties to the entity.

- **Manage Properties:** Implement property management practices to maintain and optimize the performance of the real estate assets. This includes tasks such as tenant relations, maintenance, rent collection, and financial reporting.

- **Keep Accurate Financial Records:** Maintain detailed records of income, expenses, and transactions related to real estate investments. Good record-keeping is essential for tax compliance and financial analysis.

- **File Required Tax Returns:** Fulfill tax obligations by filing annual tax returns for the entity and reporting real estate income, deductions, and capital gains or losses.

- **Review and Adjust Investment Strategy:** Regularly review the performance of your real estate portfolio and adjust your investment strategy as needed to align with changing market conditions and investment objectives.

Although incorporating a property can offer several advantages, it is essential to also carefully evaluate key potential implications before making a decision. Table 8 outlines some key advantages and disadvantages of incorporating a rental property.

Table 8. **Advantages and Disadvantages of Incorporating**

ADVANTAGES OF INCORPORATING	DISADVANTAGES OF INCORPORATING
Limited Liability Protection for Owners: One of the primary benefits of incorporating a real estate investment is that it provides limited liability protection to the owners (shareholders or members). This means that in the event of lawsuits or financial obligations, the personal assets of the owners are generally protected, and only the assets of the corporation or LLC are at risk.	**Higher Administrative and Legal Costs**: Establishing and maintaining a corporation or LLC typically involves higher administrative and legal costs compared to owning real estate personally. There may be fees associated with incorporation, ongoing compliance requirements, and the need for professional services such as legal and accounting assistance.
Potential Tax Benefits: Incorporating a real estate investment can offer various tax advantages. For example, both corporations and LLCs may be able to deduct expenses such as mortgage interest, property taxes, and depreciation. Additionally, certain structures, such as pass-through entities like LLCs, allow profits and losses to flow through to the owners' personal tax returns, potentially reducing overall tax liability.	**Complex Regulatory Requirements**: Corporations and LLCs are subject to various regulatory requirements at the federal, state, and local levels. Compliance with regulations such as filing annual reports, holding shareholder meetings, and maintaining corporate records can be complex and time-consuming.
Ability to Raise Capital: Corporations, particularly publicly traded REITs, have the ability to raise capital by selling shares of stock to investors. This can provide a significant source of funding for real estate acquisitions, developments, or expansions.	**Loss of Some Tax Benefits Compared to Direct Ownership**: While incorporating a real estate investment can offer tax advantages, there may be limitations or restrictions on certain deductions or tax benefits compared to owning real estate directly. For example, some tax benefits may be subject to passive activity rules or limitations on deductions for high-income earners.
Separation of Personal and Business Assets: By incorporating a real estate investment, owners can separate their personal assets from those of the business entity. This separation can provide added protection for personal assets in the event of legal issues or financial difficulties faced by the corporation or LLC.	**Limited Flexibility in Decision-Making**: Incorporating a real estate investment introduces a corporate governance structure, which may limit the flexibility of decision-making compared to owning real estate personally. Shareholders or members may have to abide by corporate bylaws, voting requirements, or approval processes for certain actions.
Enhanced Credibility and Professionalism: Incorporating a real estate investment can enhance its credibility and professionalism in the eyes of lenders, investors, and tenants. Operating as a formal business entity may instill confidence and attract more favorable financing terms or investment opportunities.	**Potential for Double Taxation (for C Corporations)**: If a real estate investment is structured as a C corporation, there is a risk of double taxation. C corporations are subject to corporate income tax on their profits, and if dividends are distributed to shareholders, those dividends may be taxed again at the individual level. This can result in higher overall tax liability compared to pass-through entities like LLCs.

Here is a case study about Sarah, who is exploring the process of incorporating her rental property investment:

Case Study: SARAH

» ***Investor Profile:***
Name: Sarah
Occupation: Software Engineer
Investment Experience: Moderate
Portfolio: Three single-family rental properties

» ***Objective:*** Sarah aims to protect her personal assets, optimize tax obligations, and streamline property management by incorporating her rental property business.

» ***Decision-Making Process:***
Step 1: UNDERSTANDING THE BENEFITS
- Liability Protection: Incorporation separates personal and business assets, limiting Sarah's liability to the corporation's assets.
- Tax Advantages: Potential for tax deductions on business expenses, including mortgage interest, property management fees, and repairs.
- Operational Efficiency: Easier to manage properties under a single corporate entity, enhancing organizational structure and financial tracking.

Step 2: CHOOSING THE RIGHT BUSINESS STRUCTURE
- Sarah considered various business structures:
- Sole Proprietorship: Simple but offers no liability protection.
- Partnership: Involves sharing control and profits with partners, which wasn't relevant for Sarah.
- Corporation (C-Corp or S-Corp): Offers liability protection but comes with double taxation in the case of C-Corp.
- Limited Liability Company (LLC): Provides liability protection, pass-through taxation, and operational flexibility.
- Sarah decided to form an LLC due to its balance of liability protection, tax benefits, and administrative simplicity.

Step 3: CONSULTING PROFESSIONALS

- Sarah consulted a real estate attorney and a tax advisor to ensure her incorporation decision was legally sound and tax-efficient.

» ***Implementation:***

Step 1: FORMING THE LLC

- Name Registration: Chose a unique name for the LLC, "Sarah Rental Properties LLC."
- Filing Articles of Organization: Filed necessary paperwork with the state's Secretary of State office.
- Operating Agreement: Drafted an operating agreement outlining the LLC's management structure, member responsibilities, and financial arrangements.
- EIN Application: Obtained an EIN from the IRS for tax purposes.

Step 2: TRANSFERRING PROPERTIES TO THE LLC

- Property Titles: Transferred the titles of her rental properties to the LLC, ensuring all future transactions are under the LLC's name.
- Bank Accounts: Opened separate bank accounts for the LLC to segregate personal and business finances.
- Insurance Policies: Updated insurance policies to reflect the LLC as the property owner, ensuring appropriate coverage.

Step 3: FINANCIAL MANAGEMENT

- Bookkeeping: Implemented accounting software to manage income, expenses, and financial reporting for the LLC.
- Tax Filings: Coordinated with her tax advisor to ensure proper tax filings, including quarterly estimated tax payments and annual returns.

» ***Outcomes:***

- Liability Protection: Sarah successfully insulated her personal assets from potential liabilities arising from her rental properties. In case of lawsuits or creditor claims, only the LLC's assets are at risk.
- Tax Optimization: Sarah benefited from pass-through taxation, avoiding double taxation and allowing her to claim business expense deductions. Her tax advisor identified further tax-saving opportunities, such as depreciation.

- Operational Efficiency: Managing her properties became more stream-lined. The LLC structure facilitated better financial tracking, simplified transactions, and provided a clear organizational framework.
- Professional Growth: Incorporating her rental business enhanced Sarah's professional credibility. She was better positioned to negotiate with lenders, contractors, and tenants.

» ***Challenges:***
- Administrative Burden: Initial setup required significant time and effort, including paperwork and professional consultations.
- Cost: Legal and consulting fees, filing fees, and ongoing compliance costs added to the investment expenses.

» ***Lessons Learned:***
- Professional Advice: Consulting with legal and tax professionals is crucial to navigating the complexities of incorporation.
- Ongoing Compliance: Regular compliance with state and federal regulations is essential to maintain the benefits of incorporation.
- Financial Discipline: Maintaining separate finances and detailed records is critical for legal protection and tax efficiency.

» ***Conclusion:*** Incorporating her rental property business as an LLC provided Sarah with substantial benefits, including liability protection, tax advantages, and improved operational efficiency. Despite initial challenges, the decision proved to be financially and strategically sound. This case study demonstrates the importance of thorough planning, professional advice, and diligent management in the successful incorporation of a rental property investment business.

Ultimately, whether to incorporate your real estate investment property depends on your individual circumstances, risk tolerance, long-term financial goals, liability protection, taxation, management preferences, estate planning, and the number of owners involved. It is essential to carefully weigh all potential advantages and disadvantages and consult with legal and financial professionals to make an informed decision.

Advantages and disadvantages of incorporating a real estate investment:

ADVANTAGES:

- Limited liability protection for owners.
- Potential tax benefits such as depreciation deductions and mortgage interest deductions.
- Ability to raise capital through equity financing.
- Separation of personal and business assets.
- Enhanced credibility and professionalism.

DISADVANTAGES:

- Higher administrative and legal costs associated with incorporation.
- Complex regulatory requirements and compliance obligations.
- Loss of some tax benefits compared to direct ownership.
- Limited flexibility in decision-making due to corporate governance structure.
- Potential for double taxation if structured as a C corporation.

CHAPTER 7
THE SEVEN R'S™

"Don't wait to buy real estate, buy real estate and wait."

—T. HARV EKER, author and motivational speaker

In numerology, the number seven represents a pursuit of introspection and knowledge. The number seven is also significant in some major religions, symbolizing the seven days of completion or perfection and the seven main chakras in the human body. There are seven continents on planet Earth, seven days in a week, and even a rainbow has seven colors. No other number has so many references and connotations in so many different fields like the number seven. Similarly, there are seven major steps when building a rental property investment portfolio. Those seven steps are **R**ental property purchase, **R**enovate, **R**ent, **R**etain, **R**efinance, **R**einvest, and **R**epeat. This cycle of seven, which I call the Seven R's™, depicts the blueprint that many investors use to expand their real estate holdings.

By adhering to this blueprint, shown in Figure 3, investors can systematically grow their real estate portfolios, increase cash flow, and build long-term wealth. However, it requires careful planning, market analysis, and financial management to execute successfully.

Figure 3. **Seven R′s™**

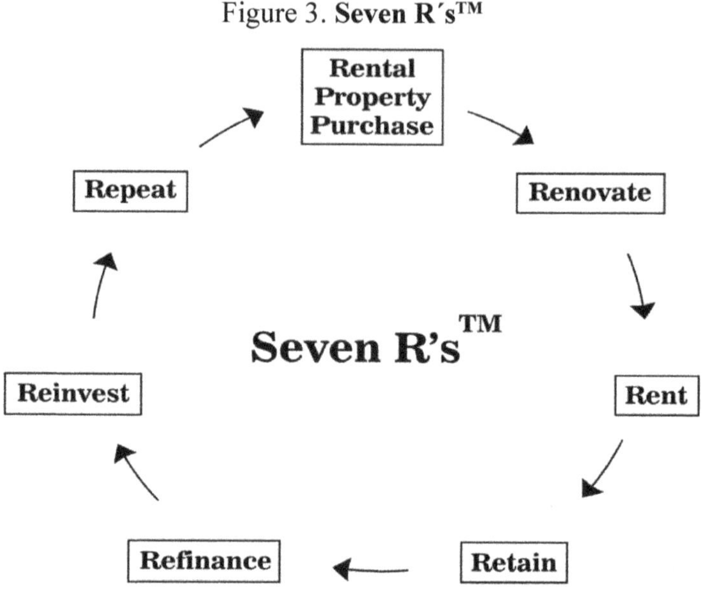

7.1 Rental Property Purchase

The first step in the Seven R's™ is "Rental Property Purchase." The entire process of purchasing a rental property has been previously discussed in full detail in Chapter 5: "The CAP Tripod™." Real estate purchase in rental property investing involves acquiring properties with the primary intention of renting them out to generate income. This strategy requires careful consideration of several key factors.

First, location is crucial; properties in desirable neighborhoods with access to amenities, good schools, and transportation are likely to attract more tenants and command higher rents. Second, financial analysis is essential to determine potential returns. Investors must calculate expected rental income, property taxes, insurance, maintenance costs, and mortgage payments to assess the profitability of the investment. Understanding local market trends and vacancy rates can also provide insights into the property's potential performance. Additionally, securing financing is a critical step, often involving obtaining a mortgage or leveraging existing equity. Investors should also be aware of legal requirements, such as landlord-tenant laws and zoning regulations, which vary by location.

Proper property management, either self-managed or through a professional service, ensures that the property remains in good condition and tenants are satisfied, thereby sustaining rental income. By meticulously evaluating these aspects, investors can make informed decisions, mitigate risks, and maximize their returns in the rental property market.

Some key factors to keep in mind when purchasing a rental investment property are:

- **Define Your Investment Goals:** Determine your investment objectives, such as generating rental income, building equity, or diversifying your investment portfolio. Understanding your goals will help guide your property search and investment strategy.

- **Research the Market:** Conduct thorough market research to identify potential investment opportunities. Analyze factors such as property values, rental rates, vacancy rates, local economic conditions, employment trends, and demographic trends in the area.

- **Set a Budget:** Determine your budget for purchasing a rental property, including the down payment, closing costs, ongoing maintenance expenses, property management fees, and reserves for unexpected expenses. Be realistic about your financial capabilities and consider seeking pre-approval for financing if necessary.

- **Identify Suitable Properties:** Look for properties that align with your investment goals and budget. Consider factors such as location, property type (single-family home, multi-family property, condominium, etc.), condition of the property, potential for rental income, and appreciation potential.

- **Conduct Due Diligence:** Perform thorough due diligence on potential investment properties before making an offer. This includes inspecting the property for any issues or repairs needed, reviewing financial documents (such as rental history, operating expenses, and tax records), and analyzing the potential ROI.

- **Understand Financing Options:** Explore different financing options for purchasing a rental property, such as conventional mortgages, FHA loans, VA loans (if you qualify), private financing, or cash purchases. Compare interest rates, terms, down payment requirements, and eligibility criteria to choose the best option for your needs.

- **Calculate Potential Returns:** Estimate the potential returns on investment for each property you're considering. This includes analyzing rental income potential, operating expenses (such as property taxes, insurance, maintenance, utilities, and property management fees), and potential appreciation in property value over time.

- **Consider Property Management:** Decide whether you'll manage the property yourself or hire a professional property management company to handle day-to-day operations, tenant screening, rent collection, maintenance, and repairs. Factor property management costs into your budget and investment calculations.

- **Review Legal and Regulatory Considerations:** Familiarize yourself with landlord-tenant laws, zoning regulations, building codes, and other legal and regulatory requirements that apply to rental properties in your area. Ensure compliance with all applicable laws and obtain any necessary permits or licenses.

- **Plan for Contingencies:** Be prepared for unexpected challenges or expenses that may arise during the ownership of the property, such as vacancies, tenant turnover, property damage, or economic downturns. Maintain reserves to cover these contingencies and mitigate risks to your investment.

- **Seek Professional Advice:** Consider consulting with real estate agents, attorneys, financial advisors, and other professionals who specialize in real estate investing. Their expertise and guidance can help you navigate the purchasing process and make informed decisions about your investment.

By understanding these key considerations and thoroughly researching potential investment properties, you can make informed decisions and set yourself up for success as a rental property investor.

7.2 Renovate

The second step in the Seven R's™ is "Renovate." Renovating a rental property is a strategic approach to enhance the property's appeal, increase its value, and attract higher-paying tenants. This process begins with a thorough assessment of the property's current condition to identify areas that require improvement, ranging from cosmetic updates like fresh paint and new flooring to significant upgrades such as kitchen and bathroom remodels, electrical and plumbing systems, and energy-efficient installations.

Investors must balance the cost of renovations with the potential increase in rental income and property value, ensuring that the upgrades provide a good ROI. Prioritizing renovations that offer the highest impact, such as modernizing kitchens and bathrooms, improving curb appeal, and adding desirable amenities like in-unit laundry or upgraded appliances, can make the property more competitive in the rental market.

Additionally, quality renovations can reduce maintenance issues and attract long-term tenants, thereby reducing vacancy rates and turnover costs. It is crucial to adhere to local building codes and regulations during the renovation process and consider hiring licensed professionals for specialized tasks to ensure the work is done correctly and safely.

By carefully planning and executing renovations, investors can significantly enhance the attractiveness and profitability of their rental properties.

However, it is essential to approach renovations thoughtfully and consider the following factors:

- **Understand Your Target Market:** Before embarking on renovations, research your target rental market to understand the preferences and needs of potential tenants. Tailor your renovations to appeal to your target demographic, whether it's families, young professionals, students, or retirees.

- **Focus on High-Impact Areas:** Prioritize renovations that will have the most significant impact on the property's value and appeal to tenants. Focus on essential areas such as kitchens, bathrooms, flooring, and curb appeal to attract renters and command higher rents.

- **Set a Realistic Budget:** Determine your renovation budget and stick to it. Factor in the cost of materials, labor, permits, and any unforeseen expenses that may arise during the renovation process. Be realistic about what you can afford and avoid over-improving the property for the rental market.

- **Consider ROI:** Evaluate the potential return on investment for each renovation project. Focus on renovations that offer the highest ROI, such as kitchen and bathroom upgrades, energy-efficient improvements, and cosmetic enhancements that add value without breaking the bank.

- **Choose Durable Materials:** Opt for durable, low-maintenance materials that can withstand the wear and tear of rental living. Choose flooring, countertops, fixtures, and appliances that are both stylish and practical, minimizing the need for frequent repairs and replacements.

- **Comply with Building Codes and Regulations:** Ensure that all renovation work complies with local building codes, zoning regulations, and safety standards. Obtain any necessary permits before starting renovation projects to avoid fines or delays.

- **Focus on Functionality:** Prioritize functionality and practicality in your renovation plans. Create functional living spaces that meet the needs of tenants, with ample storage, efficient layouts, and modern amenities that enhance the overall quality of life.

- **Enhance Energy Efficiency:** Consider incorporating energy-efficient upgrades into your renovation plans, such as installing energy-efficient appliances, LED lighting, programmable thermostats, and improving insulation. Not only can these upgrades attract environmentally conscious tenants, but they can also lower utility costs and improve the property's sustainability.

- **Invest in Safety and Security:** Prioritize safety and security enhancements to protect your tenants and minimize liability risks. Install smoke detectors, carbon monoxide detectors, fire extinguishers, secure locks, and outdoor lighting to ensure a safe living environment for tenants.

- **Consult Professionals:** Consider hiring experienced contractors, architects, designers, and other professionals to assist with the renovation process. Their expertise can help ensure that renovations are completed to a high standard, on time, and within budget.

- **Communicate with Tenants:** If the property is currently occupied, communicate with tenants about upcoming renovations, potential disruptions, and any changes that may affect their living arrangements. Be respectful of their needs and concerns throughout the renovation process.

By carefully planning and executing renovations, you can enhance the value and appeal of your rental investment property, attract quality tenants, and achieve long-term success as a real estate investor.

7.3 Rent

The third step in the Seven R's™ is "Rent." Successfully renting out a property involves meticulous planning, strategic marketing, and effective management to ensure continuous occupancy and steady rental income.

The process starts with preparing the property by ensuring it is in excellent condition, which includes thorough cleaning, making necessary repairs, and possibly upgrading features to enhance its appeal to prospective tenants. Setting a competitive rental price is crucial; this involves researching the local rental market to understand current rates and adjusting for the property's unique features and location advantages.

Marketing the property effectively is key to attracting potential tenants; this can be achieved through high-quality photographs, detailed and engaging property descriptions, and listings on popular rental platforms and social media channels. The tenant screening process is critical to ensure reliable and responsible tenants; this typically includes background checks, credit checks, employment verification, and rental history reviews. Crafting a clear and comprehensive lease agreement that outlines all terms and conditions, including rent amount, payment schedule, maintenance responsibilities, and property rules, helps prevent misunderstandings and legal issues.

Once the property is rented, maintaining open communication with tenants and responding promptly to maintenance requests fosters a positive landlord-tenant relationship and encourages lease renewals. Regular property inspections and proactive maintenance help preserve the property's condition and value. By following these steps, landlords can achieve successful and profitable rental operations. When looking for tenants for a rental investment property, there are several important factors to consider to attract quality tenants and ensure a successful rental experience:

- **Understand Your Target Market:** Identify your target rental market based on factors such as location, property type, amenities, and rental rates. Tailor your marketing efforts to appeal to your target demographic, whether it's families, young professionals, students, or retirees.

- **Prepare the Property:** Ensure that the rental property is clean, well-maintained, and in good condition before showing it to prospective tenants. Make any necessary repairs or improvements to enhance its appeal and maximize rental value.

- **Set Competitive Rent:** Research local rental market trends to determine a competitive rental rate for your property. Price the rent appropriately based on factors such as location, size, amenities, and comparable properties in the area.

- **Market the Property:** Utilize various marketing channels to advertise the rental property and attract potential tenants. This may include online listing platforms, social media, rental websites, yard signs, local newspapers, and word-of-mouth referrals.

- **Create Compelling Listings:** Write detailed and compelling rental listings that highlight the features, amenities, and benefits of the property. Include high-quality photos and accurate descriptions to attract the attention of prospective tenants.

- **Screen Tenants Thoroughly:** Implement a rigorous tenant screening process to evaluate prospective tenants' credit history, rental history, income verification, employment status, and references. Screen tenants consistently and fairly to ensure compliance with fair housing laws.

- **Use Rental Applications:** Require prospective tenants to complete a rental application providing relevant personal and financial information. Review the applications carefully to assess each tenant's suitability and make informed leasing decisions.

- **Establish Clear Rental Criteria:** Define clear rental criteria based on factors such as credit score requirements, income-to-rent ratio, rental history, and background checks. Communicate your rental criteria to prospective tenants upfront to manage expectations and streamline the screening process.

- **Create a Lease Agreement:** Draft a comprehensive lease agreement that outlines the terms and conditions of the rental agreement, including rent amount, lease duration, security deposit, pet policies, maintenance responsibilities, and other relevant provisions. Consult with a legal professional to ensure that the lease complies with local laws and regulations.

- **Communicate Expectations:** Clearly communicate your expectations to tenants regarding rent payments, maintenance requests, property rules, and other important policies. Establish open lines of communication and address any questions or concerns promptly to foster a positive landlord-tenant relationship.

- **Provide Excellent Customer Service:** Provide responsive and attentive customer service to tenants throughout the leasing process and during their tenancy. Address maintenance issues promptly, respect tenants' privacy, and strive to create a comfortable and enjoyable living environment.

By following these guidelines and taking a proactive approach to tenant screening and property management, you can attract quality tenants, minimize vacancies, and maintain a successful rental investment property.

7.4 Retain

The fourth step in the Seven R's™ is "Retain." Holding or retaining a rental investment property for a period of time offers numerous financial and strategic benefits.

One of the primary advantages of retaining a property for a while is the potential for long-term capital appreciation. As property values typically increase over time, the investor can build substantial equity, enhancing their overall net worth. Consistent rental income provides a steady cash flow, which can be used to cover mortgage payments, property maintenance, and other expenses, often leading to positive cash flow and passive income.

Additionally, holding onto the property allows investors to benefit from tax advantages such as depreciation deductions, which can significantly reduce taxable income. Over time, rents can be increased to keep pace with inflation and market rates, further boosting income. Long-term ownership also enables investors to weather market fluctuations, avoiding the need to sell during downturns and potentially maximizing profits by selling during peak market conditions. Moreover, maintaining the property for a longer period allows for gradual improvements and renovations, which can enhance the property's value and rental appeal without incurring significant upfront costs.

Retaining the property also provides stability and the opportunity to establish strong relationships with tenants, leading to lower turnover rates and reduced vacancy periods. Overall, holding a rental investment property long-term can lead to increased financial security, growth in wealth, and a more stable investment portfolio. Some of the key advantages include:

- **Steady Rental Income:** One of the primary benefits of holding a rental investment property is the steady stream of rental income it can generate. Rental income provides a reliable source of cash flow that can help cover mortgage payments and property expenses and generate passive income for the property owner.

- **Appreciation in Property Value:** Over time, rental investment properties have the potential to appreciate in value, especially in areas with strong economic growth and increasing demand for real estate. Property appreciation can result in capital gains when the property is sold, allowing investors to realize a profit on their investment.

- **Equity Buildup:** As tenants pay down the mortgage over time, property owners build equity in the rental property. Equity represents the difference between the property's market value and the remaining mortgage balance. Accumulating equity provides investors with financial leverage and opportunities for future investments or financing options.

- **Tax Benefits:** Rental investment properties offer several tax advantages for property owners. These may include deductions for mortgage interest, property taxes, insurance premiums, maintenance expenses, depreciation, and other eligible expenses. Additionally, investors may benefit from capital gains tax treatment upon the sale of the property.

- **Inflation Hedge:** Real estate is often considered an effective hedge against inflation. As inflation erodes the value of currency over time, real assets like rental properties tend to retain or increase in value, providing a measure of protection against purchasing power erosion.

- **Diversification of Portfolio:** Holding rental investment properties can diversify an investor's portfolio and reduce overall investment risk. Real estate investments have a low correlation with traditional financial assets like stocks and bonds, offering added diversification benefits and potentially reducing portfolio volatility.

- **Control Over Investment:** Unlike some other investment vehicles, rental properties provide investors with a high degree of control over their investment. Property owners can make strategic decisions regarding property management, renovations, rental pricing, and tenant selection to maximize returns and mitigate risks.

- **Passive Income and Wealth Building:** Rental investment properties offer the opportunity to generate passive income and build wealth over time. By holding onto properties for an extended period and allowing rental income and property appreciation to accumulate, investors can achieve long-term financial stability and achieve their wealth-building goals.

Holding a rental investment property for a period of time allows investors to benefit from ongoing rental income, property appreciation, tax advantages, and wealth accumulation, making it a valuable component of a diversified investment portfolio.

7.5 Refinance

The fifth step in the Seven R's™ is "Refinance." When building your rental property investment portfolio, a cash-out refinance is the name of the game. Depending on individual financial goals and circumstances, it offers several advantages for property owners.

A cash-out refinance with a rental investment property offers several strategic financial benefits for investors. This process involves refinancing the existing mortgage and taking out a new loan for a higher amount, with the difference provided as cash to the property owner. One of the primary advantages is access to a significant amount of capital, which can be used to invest in additional properties, thereby expanding the investor's portfolio and potentially increasing overall rental income and diversification.

The funds can also be used for property improvements and renovations, which can enhance the property's value and attract higher-paying tenants, leading to increased rental income. Moreover, a cash-out refinance can be an effective way to consolidate high-interest debt, using the proceeds to pay off credit cards or other loans, thus reducing overall interest expenses and improving cash flow. Since mortgage interest rates are typically lower than other types of loans, this strategy can result in significant savings. Additionally, mortgage interest is usually tax-deductible, providing further financial benefits.

By leveraging the built-up equity in the property, investors can optimize their investment strategy, improve liquidity, and better position themselves for future opportunities without the need to liquidate existing assets. This approach not only enhances the financial flexibility of the investor but also maximizes the potential returns on their rental property investment.

The process of a cash-out refinance involves a few major steps:

1. Determine Property Value and Existing Mortgage Balance:
- Appraised Value: This is the current market value of your rental property.
- Existing Mortgage Balance: This is how much you still owe on your current mortgage.

2. Choose New Loan Amount:
- Lenders typically allow you to refinance up to a certain percentage of your property's appraised value (usually 70%–80% for rental properties).

3. Calculate Available Cash:
- Subtract the existing mortgage balance from the new loan amount. The difference is the cash you can take out.

4. Close the Loan and Receive Cash:
- You close on the new loan, which pays off your old mortgage and gives you the remaining amount in cash.

Here is an example of a cash-out refinance:

Details of the Rental Property:
- Appraised Value of Rental Property: $500,000
- Existing Mortgage Balance: $200,000
- Loan-to-Value (LTV) Ratio Allowed by Lender: 75%

Step 1: Determine New Loan Amount
- Maximum Loan Amount = Appraised Value × LTV Ratio
- Maximum Loan Amount = $500,000 × 75% = $375,000

Step 2: Calculate Available Cash
- New Loan Amount: $375,000
- Existing Mortgage Balance: $200,000
- Available Cash = New Loan Amount − Existing Mortgage Balance
- Available Cash = $375,000 - $200,000 = $175,000

Step 3: Close the Loan and Receive Cash
- You refinance your mortgage with a new loan of $375,000.
- The lender pays off your existing mortgage of $200,000.
- You receive $175,000 in cash at closing.

The $175,000 proceeds from the cash-out refinance can be used for:

Property Improvements:
- Use the $175,000 to renovate the rental property, potentially increasing its value and rental income.
- Example: Renovate the kitchen and bathrooms, add energy-efficient appliances, or upgrade the landscaping.

Purchasing Additional Properties:

- Use the cash as a down payment for another rental property to expand your portfolio.
- Example: Buy a new rental property worth $500,000 with a 20% down payment ($100,000) and use the remaining $75,000 for closing costs and initial repairs.

Debt Consolidation:

- Pay off higher-interest debts to improve your financial situation.
- Example: Pay off $50,000 in credit card debt and $50,000 in personal loans, reducing your overall interest expenses. Use the remaining $75,000 as a down payment for a new rental property.

Other Investments:

- Invest in other areas such as stocks, bonds, or starting a business.
- Example: Use $75,000 to invest in a diversified stock portfolio and $100,000 to start a small business.

However, there are some considerations to keep in mind when doing a cash-out refinance:

1. Interest Rates:

- Interest rates for rental property loans are generally higher than for primary residences.
- Your new interest rate could impact your monthly payments and overall cost of the loan.

2. Loan Costs:

- There are costs associated with refinancing, such as closing costs, appraisal fees, and potentially higher interest rates.

3. Impact on Cash Flow:

- While you get a lump sum of cash, your monthly mortgage payments will likely increase due to the larger loan amount.

4. Tax Implications:

- The interest on a cash-out refinance for a rental property is generally tax-deductible as it is considered investment interest.
- Consult a tax advisor to understand the specific implications of your situation.

A cash-out refinance on a rental property can be a powerful financial tool if used wisely. It can be a useful strategy for leveraging the equity in your rental property to access funds for investment opportunities or other financial goals. However, it is crucial to weigh the potential benefits against the risks and ensure that the decision aligns with your overall investment strategy and financial objectives. Consulting with a financial advisor or mortgage professional can provide personalized guidance based on your specific circumstances.

7.6 Reinvest

The sixth step in the Seven R's™ is "Reinvest." Once you have completed the cash-out refinance, the goal is to then take the cash that you received from the refinance and use it as a down payment to purchase your next rental investment property. Reinvesting the money to purchase additional rental investment properties can significantly enhance an investor's portfolio and overall wealth-building strategy. By leveraging the equity in an existing property, investors can access substantial capital without liquidating assets, allowing them to acquire more properties and diversify their holdings.

This expansion can lead to increased rental income streams, providing greater cash flow stability and reducing the risk associated with relying on a single property. Additionally, acquiring multiple properties in different locations or types, such as single-family homes, multi-family units, or commercial properties, can further mitigate risk and capitalize on varying market trends. The increased number of properties also offers more opportunities for long-term capital appreciation, as each property can individually grow in value over time.

Moreover, the economies of scale become more pronounced with a larger portfolio; management costs can be distributed across multiple properties, potentially reducing per-unit expenses. Tax benefits are also amplified, as investors can take advantage of depreciation and other deductions across a broader range of assets. This reinvestment strategy not only enhances income potential and asset diversification but also strengthens the investor's market presence and financial resilience, creating a robust foundation for sustained growth and long-term success in the rental property market and contributing to long-term financial growth and wealth accumulation. Some of the key advantages of reinvesting funds to purchase additional rental properties are:

- **Capital Growth:** Reinvesting funds in additional rental investment properties allows property owners to leverage their existing capital to acquire more assets. Over time, the value of the investment portfolio can increase through property appreciation, rental income growth, and equity buildup, leading to capital growth and increased net worth.

- **Diversification:** Investing in multiple rental properties helps diversify an investor's real estate portfolio, spreading risk across different properties, locations, and market segments. Diversification can reduce overall investment risk and mitigate the impact of negative market trends or fluctuations in individual properties.

- **Passive Income:** Acquiring additional rental properties generates additional streams of passive income through rental payments from tenants. The combined rental income from multiple properties can enhance cash flow, provide financial stability, and supplement other sources of income for the property owner.

- **Scale and Efficiency:** Reinvesting funds in rental properties allows investors to scale their real estate portfolio and achieve economies of scale. With a larger portfolio, property owners can spread fixed costs over more properties, negotiate better terms with suppliers and service providers, and increase operational efficiency, leading to higher profitability.

- **Tax Benefits:** Owning multiple rental properties provides opportunities for tax advantages and deductions that can lower overall tax liability. These may include deductions for mortgage interest, property taxes, depreciation, maintenance expenses, and other eligible expenses associated with owning and operating rental properties.

- **Appreciation Potential:** Each additional rental property acquired through reinvestment has the potential to appreciate in value over time, increasing the investor's overall portfolio value. Property appreciation can result from factors such as market demand, economic growth, property improvements, and inflation, leading to long-term wealth accumulation.

- **Wealth Building:** Reinvesting funds in rental investment properties is a powerful wealth-building strategy that allows investors to leverage their initial capital to acquire appreciating assets and generate passive income over time. With disciplined reinvestment and strategic property acquisitions, investors can achieve significant wealth accumulation and financial independence.

- **Hedge Against Inflation:** Real estate investments, particularly rental properties, can serve as an effective hedge against inflation. As inflation erodes the value of currency over time, real assets like rental properties tend to retain or increase in value, providing a measure of protection against purchasing power erosion.

Reinvesting funds from a cash-out refinance in more rental properties can provide property owners with opportunities for capital growth, diversification, passive income, tax benefits, and long-term wealth building. However, it is essential to conduct thorough due diligence, assess investment risks, and develop a strategic investment plan to maximize the benefits of reinvestment and achieve financial goals.

7.7 Repeat

The seventh and final step in the Seven R's[TM] is "Repeat." After you have reinvested the funds from the cash-out refinance to purchase another rental property, you basically repeat the cycle all over again. The term "repeat" in real estate typically refers to the action of an investor acquiring additional investment properties after having already purchased one or more properties previously. It simply implies a pattern of behavior where an investor engages in multiple property acquisitions over time. Here are a few ways "repeat" is relevant in real estate investing:

- **Repeat Investors:** A "repeat investor" is someone who has previously invested in real estate and is now considering additional property acquisitions. These investors have experience with the process and may be more comfortable and confident in expanding their real estate portfolio.

- **Repeat Purchases:** When an investor decides to acquire another investment property after already owning one or more properties, it's referred to as a "repeat purchase." This could involve buying similar types of properties or diversifying into different property types or locations.

- **Repeat Investment Strategies:** Investors may employ "repeat" investment strategies, where they replicate successful approaches or techniques used in previous property acquisitions. This could include targeting specific markets, property types, financing methods, or renovation strategies that have proven effective in the past.

- **Repeat Transactions:** In real estate transactions, "repeat" can refer to repeat business between investors and other parties involved in the process, such as real estate agents, lenders, contractors, or property managers. Establishing ongoing relationships with trusted professionals can facilitate smoother transactions and lead to mutually beneficial outcomes.

Repeating the process of buying a rental property, conducting a cash-out refinance, and then reinvesting the money to purchase additional rental properties can significantly accelerate wealth accumulation and portfolio growth for real estate investors.

Initially, the investor purchases a rental property, often one that is undervalued or requires improvements. After acquiring the property, they undertake renovations to increase its market value and rental income potential. Once the property is rented out and generates steady cash flow, the investor applies for a cash-out refinance, leveraging the increased equity resulting from the appreciation and improvements. The cash obtained from the refinance is then used to acquire another rental property, starting the cycle anew. This strategy enables investors to continually scale their portfolios without needing substantial upfront capital for each new purchase.

By reinvesting the proceeds from each cash-out refinance, investors can rapidly expand their holdings, diversify risk across multiple properties, and enhance overall rental income. Additionally, the repeated cycle allows for continuous optimization of the portfolio, as each newly acquired property can be strategically chosen to complement and strengthen the investor's existing assets. The compounding effect of this strategy, coupled with prudent property management and market analysis, can lead to exponential growth in both net worth and passive income streams over time, establishing a robust and resilient real estate investment portfolio.

Below is a case study about Sarah, and how she used a cash-out refinance to expand her rental property portfolio:

Case Study: Sarah

> » **Background:** Sarah, an experienced real estate investor, owned a rental property in a desirable urban neighborhood. The property had appreciated significantly since she purchased it, and Sarah saw an opportunity to leverage this equity to expand her real estate portfolio.

» **Strategy:** Sarah assessed the current market value of her rental property and compared it to the remaining mortgage balance to determine the available equity. She conducted a thorough financial analysis to evaluate the potential cash flow and returns of acquiring another rental property using the cash-out refinance proceeds. Sarah then researched different lenders and mortgage options to find the most favorable terms for a cash-out refinance that would provide her with the necessary funds for the new investment. After selecting a lender, Sarah applied for a cash-out refinance loan, providing documentation of her rental income, creditworthiness, and property value. Following a review process, her application was approved, and she received the funds. With the cash from the refinance, Sarah identified a promising investment property in a nearby up-and-coming neighborhood. She conducted due diligence on the property, including inspections and financial analysis, before finalizing the purchase. Sarah focused on effective property management for both her existing rental property and the newly acquired one. This included tenant screening, rent collection, property maintenance, and ongoing financial monitoring.

» **Outcome:** By leveraging the equity in her existing rental property, Sarah was able to acquire another property without using her own savings or taking on additional debt beyond the cash-out refinance loan. The acquisition of the new rental property diversified Sarah's investment portfolio, spreading her risk across multiple properties and potentially increasing her overall returns. Both properties generated rental income, contributing to positive cash flow. Additionally, as property values continued to appreciate over time, Sarah's equity in both properties increased, further enhancing her net worth.

» **Lesson Learned:** Sarah's case underscores the importance of strategically leveraging equity in real estate investments to fund additional acquisitions or investment opportunities. Thorough financial analysis and due diligence are critical when considering a cash-out refinance and the purchase of another rental property. It is essential to ensure that the new investment aligns with investment goals and has the potential to generate positive returns. Successful property management is key to maximizing returns and mitigating risks in real estate investing. Proper tenant screening, proactive maintenance, and financial monitoring are essential components of effective property management. While leveraging equity can provide opportunities for growth, investors must also consider associated risks, such as changes in market conditions, interest rates, and rental demand. Diversification and careful risk management strategies can help mitigate these risks.

Here is an illustration of how you can leverage the Seven R's™ to expand your rental property portfolio:

Figure 4. **Rental property purchase**

Figure 5. **Renovate**

Figure 6. **Rent**

Figure 7. **Retain**

Figure 8. **Refinance**

Figure 9. **Reinvest**

Figure 10. **Repeat**

The Seven R's™ to grow your rental investment property portfolio:

- Rental property purchase.
- Renovate.
- Rent.
- Retain.
- Refinance.
- Reinvest.
- Repeat.

CHAPTER 8

THE GOOD, THE BAD, THE UGLY

"Real estate is the purest form of entrepreneurship."

—BRIAN BUFFINI, Irish American real estate coach and motivational speaker

Depending on various factors and perspectives, several aspects can be considered "good," "bad," or "ugly" when investing in rental properties. Understanding these aspects can help you make informed decisions and mitigate risks in your real estate investment endeavors.

On the positive side, the good aspects include the potential for steady, passive income through rental payments, which can contribute to long-term financial stability. Additionally, real estate often appreciates over time, offering investors a profitable return on investment when they decide to sell. The ability to leverage borrowed capital to purchase properties also allows investors to expand their portfolios without needing the full amount upfront. However, the bad aspects involve the ongoing responsibilities and costs associated with property maintenance, repairs, and management, which can eat into profits and require significant time and effort. Tenant issues, such as late payments or property damage, further complicate the investment, potentially causing stress and financial strain. The ugly side of rental property investing can manifest in market volatility and economic downturns, which can lead to prolonged vacancies, decreased rental income, and even property devaluation. Legal and regulatory challenges, such as changes in landlord-tenant laws and property taxes, can also pose significant risks. Thus, while rental property investing offers promising rewards, it requires a comprehensive understanding of the market, diligent management, and preparedness for potential setbacks.

Table 9. **The Good, the Bad, the Ugly of Investing in Rental Properties**

GOOD	BAD	UGLY
Appreciation: Real estate has the potential to appreciate over time, increasing the value of your investment.	**Illiquidity:** Real estate investments can be relatively illiquid compared to stocks or bonds, meaning they cannot be easily converted to cash.	**Unexpected Expenses:** Real estate investments can be prone to unexpected expenses such as repairs, renovations, or legal fees.
Passive Income: Rental properties can generate passive income through rental payments from tenants, providing a steady cash flow.	**Maintenance and Management:** Property maintenance and management can be time-consuming and costly, especially for landlords of rental properties.	**Regulatory Risks:** Changes in zoning laws, building codes, or property regulations can impact the value and use of real estate investments.
Tax Benefits: Real estate investors can benefit from tax deductions such as mortgage interest, property taxes, and depreciation.	**Market Risks:** Real estate markets can be cyclical and subject to economic downturns, leading to fluctuations in property values and rental demand.	**Economic Downturns:** Severe economic downturns or market crashes can lead to declining property values, increased vacancies, and financial distress for investors.
Hedge against Inflation: Real estate is often seen as a hedge against inflation, as property values and rental income tend to rise with inflation.	**Financing Risks:** Dependence on financing exposes investors to risks such as interest rate changes and inability to secure favorable loan terms.	**Liability:** Real estate ownership carries potential liability risks, such as lawsuits from tenants, visitors, or regulatory agencies.
Control: Unlike some other investments, real estate offers investors a level of control over their assets, allowing them to make improvements and strategic decisions to increase value.	**Tenant Risks:** Dealing with problematic tenants, vacancies, or lease disputes can pose challenges and affect rental income.	**Limited Diversification:** Investing heavily in real estate can lack diversification, leaving investors vulnerable to sector-specific risks and market downturns.

Here are some case studies highlighting the good, the bad, and the ugly in rental property investing:

Case Study 1: THE GOOD - PROFITABLE URBAN RENTAL PROPERTY

» *Background:* Lisa, an experienced real estate investor, wanted to diversify her portfolio by investing in an urban rental property. She focused on a two-bedroom condo in a growing downtown area, priced at $450,000. The neighborhood was undergoing significant gentrification with new businesses, improved infrastructure, and rising property values.

» *Strategy:* Lisa conducted extensive research on the local real estate market, including rental demand, future development plans, and demographic trends. She secured a 30-year fixed-rate mortgage at a low interest rate and invested $30,000 in modernizing the condo, particularly focusing on high-demand features like updated appliances and smart home technology.

» *Outcome:* Lisa successfully rented the condo for $3,000 per month, resulting in a strong positive cash flow after covering mortgage payments, taxes, insurance, and maintenance costs. Over five years, the property appreciated by 35%, significantly increasing her equity. Additionally, the condo's prime location ensured a steady stream of high-quality tenants, minimizing vacancy periods.

» *Lessons Learned:*
Location is key: Investing in properties in developing urban areas with strong growth potential can lead to high returns.
Detailed market research: Comprehensive research helps in making informed decisions and identifying high-demand property features.
Quality upgrades pay off: Investing in modern amenities can attract higher-paying tenants and increase property value.

Case Study 2: THE BAD - OVERESTIMATING RENTAL INCOME

» ***Background:*** James, a novice investor, purchased a three-bedroom house in a suburban area for $320,000. He was attracted by the seemingly affordable price and the potential for high rental income based on his limited research.

» ***Strategy:*** James relied on online rental estimates without verifying local rental rates and trends. He financed the purchase with a 5-year adjustable-rate mortgage (ARM) to benefit from the lower initial interest rate. He also spent $10,000 on cosmetic upgrades, expecting to rent the property quickly at a high rate.

» ***Outcome:*** James struggled to find tenants willing to pay the high rent he anticipated. Local rental rates were lower than his estimates, leading to extended vacancy periods. When his ARM interest rate adjusted upward, his mortgage payments increased significantly, further squeezing his cash flow. After two years, he had to lower the rent substantially to attract tenants, resulting in minimal profit.

» ***Lessons Learned:***
Verify rental rates: Relying on accurate, local rental data is crucial for realistic income projections.
Be mindful of adjustable-rate mortgages: ARMs can lead to financial instability, especially if rental income expectations are not met.
Understand market trends: Thorough understanding of the local rental market can prevent overestimating potential income.

Case Study 3: THE UGLY - MISMANAGED MULTI-FAMILY PROPERTY

» ***Background:*** Rebecca inherited a ten-unit apartment building in a small town. With no prior experience in property management, she decided to manage the property herself to maximize her income.

» ***Strategy:*** Rebecca opted for a hands-off management approach to save on costs. She did minimal renovations, believing the building was in acceptable condition, and set rental prices slightly below market rate to ensure full occupancy. She also did not implement a stringent tenant screening process, aiming for quick occupancy.

» **Outcome:** The low rents attracted tenants with poor credit and rental histories. Rebecca faced frequent issues with late payments, property damage, and legal disputes over evictions. The lack of maintenance led to significant deterioration of the building, resulting in high repair costs. The constant tenant turnover increased vacancy rates and reduced her overall income. Eventually, Rebecca had to hire a professional property manager and invest heavily in repairs, significantly impacting her profits.

» **Lessons Learned:**

Professional management is valuable: Hiring a property manager can ensure better tenant screening and property maintenance.

Regular maintenance is critical: Proactive maintenance prevents costly repairs and maintains property value.

Stringent tenant screening: Implementing a thorough screening process can mitigate tenant-related issues and reduce turnover.

These case studies underscore the importance of thorough market research, careful financial planning, and effective property management in achieving success and avoiding pitfalls in rental property investing. Each example highlights the significance of informed decision-making, meticulous strategies, and ongoing oversight to navigate challenges and capitalize on opportunities in the real estate market. Successful investors often combine data-driven decision-making with proactive management to maximize their returns and minimize risks.

The good, the bad, and the ugly of a rental investment property:

GOOD:

- Passive income.
- Appreciation.
- Tax benefits.
- Portfolio diversification.
- Hedge against inflation.

BAD:

- Vacancy risk.
- Maintenance costs.
- Tenant issues.
- Financing challenges.
- Market risk.

UGLY:

- Legal liabilities.
- Property damage.
- Eviction process.
- Regulatory compliance.
- Stress and burnout.

CHAPTER 9

CHECKLIST

"Real estate is the closest thing to the proverbial pot of gold."

—ADA LOUISE HUXTABLE, American architecture critic

Embarking on the journey of investing in a rental property marks a significant milestone for any first-time investor. Amid the excitement of potential returns and the prospect of passive income, it is crucial to approach this venture with careful planning and thorough preparation. In this comprehensive checklist, I have compiled a detailed roadmap tailored specifically for first-time investors in rental properties. From conducting market research to assessing financial feasibility and navigating legal considerations, this checklist will equip you with the essential tools and knowledge needed to embark on your rental property investment journey with confidence.

1. Research and Planning:

- Define your investment goals and objectives: passive income, long-term appreciation, tax benefits, etc.
- Research real estate markets to identify potential locations for investment.
- Consider property types: single-family homes, multi-unit buildings, condos, vacation homes, etc.

- Analyze rental market trends and demand in your chosen area.
- Evaluate properties based on criteria such as condition, size, rental potential, vacancy rates, job growth, and proximity to amenities and public transportation.
- Determine your budget and financing options.

2. Financing:

- Consider purchasing in cash or through financing.
- If financing, determine your down payment amount and how much you can afford to borrow.
- Explore loan options, including conventional mortgages, FHA loans, or other financing programs.
- Compare mortgage rates and terms from multiple lenders to find the best option.
- Calculate down payment requirements and closing costs.
- Get pre-approved for a mortgage or secure financing.

3. Property Search and Analysis:

- Start searching for properties that meet your criteria.
- Explore potential rental markets: consider factors like rental demand, vacancy rates, job growth, and local amenities.
- Analyze rental rates and property values in your target area.
- Evaluate the neighborhood and consider factors like schools, amenities, crime rates, etc.
- Identify properties that meet your requirements, and estimate potential rental income, expenses, and cash flow for each property.
- Calculate the NOI and capitalization rate (CAP) of the property.
- Determine potential ROI based on your initial investment and projected cash flow.

4. Offer and Negotiation:

- Make an offer on a property that meets your criteria.
- Once the offer is accepted, conduct property inspections, or hire a professional inspector.

- Inspect the property thoroughly for any structural issues, maintenance needs, or safety concerns.
- Review financial records, including income and expenses, to ensure the property is a sound investment.
- Verify zoning regulations and any legal restrictions on renting out the property.
- Negotiate the terms of the purchase, including final price, contingencies, and closing date.
- Review the purchase agreement and consult with a real estate attorney if necessary.

5. Due Diligence:
- Conduct thorough due diligence on the property, including title searches and property surveys.
- Review property tax records, zoning regulations, and any liens or encumbrances.
- Obtain insurance quotes for the property.
- Review lease agreements and rental history if applicable.

6. Closing Preparations:
- Schedule a final walk-through of the property.
- Coordinate with your lender, real estate agent, and attorney to prepare for closing.
- Arrange for utilities to be transferred into your name.
- Secure funds for the down payment and closing costs.

7. Closing:
- Attend the closing appointment with all necessary documentation.
- Review and sign closing documents, including the mortgage, deed, and title insurance.
- Pay closing costs and the down payment.
- Obtain keys and access to the property.

8. Post-Closing Tasks:

- Transfer utilities and services into your name.
- Inspect the property to ensure it's in the expected condition.
- Set up accounting and record-keeping systems for rental income and expenses.
- Market the property for rent if it's vacant.
- Screen potential tenants and execute lease agreements.
- Establish maintenance protocols and procedures for handling tenant requests.

9. Prepare the Property for Rent:

- Make any necessary repairs or renovations to ensure the property is in good condition.
- Clean and stage the property to attract potential tenants.
- Determine rental rates based on market research and property expenses.

10. Find Tenants:

- Advertise the property through various channels, such as online listings, social media, and local classifieds.
- Screen potential tenants carefully, including running background and credit checks.
- Draft a lease agreement outlining the terms and conditions of the rental.

11. Property Management:

- Establish a system for collecting rent payments and addressing maintenance requests.
- Stay informed about landlord-tenant laws and regulations in your area.
- Keep detailed records of income and expenses related to the property for tax purposes.

12. Risk Management:

- Identify potential risks associated with rental property investment, such as vacancy, property damage, or liability.
- Implement strategies to minimize risks, such as purchasing insurance coverage and maintaining emergency funds.
- Develop contingency plans for unexpected events, such as tenant defaults or major property repairs.
- Allocate resources for emergency repairs and unforeseen expenses.

13. Monitor and Adjust:

- Regularly review the performance of your investment property, including cash flow, occupancy rates, and market trends.
- Make necessary adjustments to your rental strategy to maximize profitability and mitigate risks.
- Consider seeking professional advice from a real estate agent, property manager, or financial advisor to optimize your investment portfolio.

This checklist covers the major steps involved in searching, purchasing, and preparing a rental property for investment. Keep in mind that real estate investing can be complex, so it is important to seek advice from professionals such as real estate agents, attorneys, and financial advisors when necessary. By following this checklist, you can navigate the process of investing in a rental property with confidence and set yourself up for success as a first-time investor.

Key steps, from start to finish, when purchasing a rental investment property:

- Set investment goals and criteria.
- Determine budget and financing options.
- Research real estate markets.
- Identify potential properties.
- Conduct property inspections.
- Analyze financials (income, expenses, NOI, CAP, ROI, taxes, etc.).
- Negotiate purchase price and terms with the seller.
- Secure financing or funding.
- Perform due diligence.
- Finalize purchase agreement.
- Coordinate with title company or attorney.
- Schedule property appraisal.
- Obtain property insurance.
- Sign closing documents.
- Transfer funds and close.
- Receive keys and ownership documents.
- Notify tenants of ownership change (if applicable).
- Transfer utilities.
- Update property management agreements (if applicable).

CHAPTER 10

RESOURCES

"The best investment on Earth is earth."

—LOUIS GLICKMAN, American real estate investor and philanthropist

When purchasing a rental investment property, conducting thorough research is paramount to making informed decisions and securing a profitable investment. This chapter delves into the myriad resources available to aspiring and seasoned investors alike, offering a comprehensive guide to navigating the complex real estate landscape. From online property listing platforms and financial analysis tools to professional services and market research data, these resources provide critical insights into property values, market trends, and neighborhood dynamics. By leveraging these tools, investors can meticulously evaluate potential properties, understand financial implications, ensure legal compliance, and ultimately make strategic investments that yield substantial returns.

1. **Real Estate Agents and Brokers:**
   - ROLE: Agents and brokers specialize in real estate transactions, providing market insights, property listings, and negotiating deals on behalf of investors.
   - BENEFITS: Access to off-market properties, local market expertise, and guidance through the buying process.

2. Online Real Estate Marketplaces:
- PLATFORMS: Websites and apps like Zillow, Realtor.com, and Redfin offer extensive property listings, market data, and tools for property research and comparison.
- BENEFITS: Convenient access to nationwide property listings, historical sales data, and neighborhood information.

3. Local Property Listings and Classifieds:
- SOURCES: Local newspapers, community boards, and neighborhood associations often advertise properties for sale or rent.
- BENEFITS: Potential access to properties not listed on mainstream platforms, fostering relationships with local sellers and landlords.

4. Market Research and Data:
- SOURCES: National Association of Realtors (NAR), Local Real Estate Board, and websites like CoreLogic, and Costar.
- BENEFITS: Provides insights into property data, analytics, market insights, and national and local real estate trends.

5. Real Estate Investment Clubs and Networks:
- PURPOSE: Membership-based groups where investors share knowledge, resources, and investment opportunities.
- BENEFITS: Networking, educational seminars, joint ventures, and access to off-market deals through peer connections.

6. Mortgage Lenders and Financial Institutions:
- PROVIDERS: Banks, credit unions, and mortgage brokers offer financing options tailored to real estate investments.
- BENEFITS: Competitive loan rates, pre-approval services, and specialized loan products such as investment property mortgages.

7. Financial Analysis Tools:
- PLATFORMS: Websites and apps, such as Rentometer, Sachdeo.com (scan QR code on page 179 for free real estate calculators), Stessa, and Property Fixer, to analyze rental income and cash flow.

- BENEFITS: Calculate potential ROI and track rental property finances, cash flow, income, and expenses.

8. Investment Analysis Tools:

- PLATFORMS: Websites such as DealCheck and Real Estate Financial Modeling (REFM) tools for financial modeling and investment analysis.
- BENEFITS: Analyze property deals, calculate ROI, and provide detailed investment reports.

9. Property Management Companies:

- SERVICES: Professional management firms handle day-to-day operations, tenant relations, maintenance, and rent collection.
- BENEFITS: Outsourcing property management tasks, maximizing rental income, and ensuring compliance with local regulations.

10. Property Management Software:

- PLATFORMS: Websites and apps, such as Buildium, AppFolio, and RentRedi to manage rental properties, tenants, and finances.
- BENEFITS: Offer property management solutions for residential and commercial properties.

11. Tenant Screening Services:

- PLATFORMS: Websites such as Cozy, TransUnion SmartMove, and MyRental.
- BENEFITS: Provide credit checks, background checks, rent collection services, and rental history verification.

12. Real Estate Attorneys and Legal Advisors:

- ROLE: Legal experts who provide counsel on property transactions, contracts, lease agreements, and landlord-tenant disputes.
- BENEFITS: Ensuring legal compliance, mitigating risks, and protecting investor interests through proper documentation and legal strategies.

13. Local Government Planning and Zoning Departments:
- FUNCTIONS: County Assessor's Office and departments responsible for zoning regulations, building permits, and development approvals.
- BENEFITS: Provide property tax records, ownership history, and assessed values; and offer information on zoning laws, potential development restrictions, and opportunities for property improvements or expansions.

14. Home Inspectors and Appraisers:
- PROFESSIONALS: Inspectors assess property conditions, while appraisers determine fair market values.
- BENEFITS: Identifying structural issues, estimating repair costs, and ensuring properties meet investment criteria.

15. Economic and Demographic Data Sources:
- DATA PROVIDERS: Government census reports, economic forecasts, Walk Score, and websites like NeighborhoodScout offer insights into local economic trends, population growth, and housing demand.
- BENEFITS: Data-driven investment decisions, identifying emerging markets, housing statistics, and understanding demographic shifts affecting rental demand. Detailed neighborhood data, including crime rates, school quality, and walkability.

Investing in rental properties demands a multifaceted approach. Leveraging the above resources empowers investors to optimize property performance, gain valuable insights, and navigate challenges effectively in the dynamic real estate market. These resources help with thorough due diligence and making informed decisions when looking to invest in rental properties.

Resources to consider when buying a rental property:

- Real estate agents and brokers.
- Online real estate marketplaces.
- Local property listings and classifieds.
- Real estate investment clubs and networks.
- Mortgage lenders and financial institutions.
- Property management companies.
- Real estate attorneys and legal advisors.
- Local government planning and zoning departments.
- Home inspectors and appraisers.
- Economic and demographic data sources.
- Scan QR code below for free real estate calculators.

CHAPTER 11

COMPREHENSIVE GLOSSARY

"The best time to buy a home is always five years ago."

—RAY BROWN, American real estate investor

Unlocking the door to the world of investing in rental properties often requires understanding its unique language. In this comprehensive glossary, I have highlighted some of the frequently used terms within the realm of real estate. Whether you are a seasoned investor, a prospective buyer, or simply curious about the terminology shaping property transactions, this glossary aims to demystify the jargon and empower you with the knowledge needed to navigate the dynamic landscape of real estate with confidence.

A

Addendum: A crucial document that plays a vital role in customizing and clarifying the terms of the purchase agreement between the buyer and the seller. This supplementary document can cover various aspects that are not explicitly addressed or need modification in the original purchase agreement. Addendums may include contingencies such as property inspections, financing terms, or appraisal requirements. They can also outline any additional agreements reached between the buyer and seller, such as seller concessions, repairs, or specific timelines for completing certain tasks before closing. Furthermore, addendums can address legal or regulatory matters relevant to the transaction, ensuring compliance with local laws and regulations. By providing a platform for detailed negotiations and adjustments, addendums enhance transparency and facilitate smoother transactions, reducing the likelihood of misunderstandings or disputes between the parties involved in the purchase of a rental property. An addendum can also supplement and modify the terms of a lease agreement between the landlord and the tenant, outlining specific rules or regulations not covered in the original lease, addressing unique circumstances, or incorporating additional terms agreed upon after the initial lease signing.

Agent: An agent typically refers to a licensed professional who represents buyers, sellers, landlords, or tenants in real estate transactions. Real estate agents are trained and knowledgeable about the local market, property values, and the intricacies of buying, selling, or renting real estate. Real estate agents are typically compensated through commissions, which are a percentage of the property's sale price or rental amount. This commission is typically paid by the seller in a sale transaction or by the landlord in a rental transaction. To work as a real estate agent, individuals must obtain a license from their state or jurisdiction by completing pre-licensing education, passing a licensing exam, and meeting other requirements such as background checks. Additionally, many agents choose to join professional associations such as the NAR for networking opportunities and access to resources and training.

Amortization: Amortization in real estate refers to the process of paying off a loan over time through regular, scheduled payments that include both principal and interest. It's a common method used for mortgages and other types of loans secured by real estate. Amortization allows borrowers to spread out the cost of a large purchase, like a home or an investment property, over time, making it more affordable. It also provides lenders with a predictable stream of income from interest payments. Over the course of the loan term, the borrower gradually builds equity in the property as the principal balance decreases.

Amortization Schedule: An amortization schedule outlines the specific payment amounts, the allocation of each payment toward principal and interest, and the remaining balance of the loan after each payment. This schedule is often provided to borrowers when they take out a loan, and it helps them understand how their payments will be applied over the life of the loan. Furthermore, it provides insights into the total interest paid over the life of the loan, enabling investors to make informed decisions about refinancing or selling the property to optimize their investment strategy.

Appraisal: In real estate, an appraisal is a professional assessment of the value of a property. Appraisals are typically conducted by licensed or certified appraisers who are trained to evaluate various factors that can influence a property's worth. An appraiser provides a report by doing a thorough inspection of the property and doing a fair market analysis of comparable properties in the same area. Appraisals are commonly required in real estate transactions involving mortgage financing, as lenders use them to determine whether the property provides sufficient collateral for the loan amount. However, appraisals may also be conducted for other purposes, such as estate planning, property tax assessment, divorce proceedings, refinances, and investment analysis. It is important to note that appraisals are subjective assessments based on professional judgment and analysis, and they may vary depending on the appraiser's expertise and methodology.

APR (Annual Percentage Rate): The APR is a crucial metric used to understand the true cost of borrowing funds for a mortgage loan. It represents the total annual cost of borrowing, including both the interest rate and any additional fees or charges associated with the loan, expressed as a percentage of the loan amount. The APR provides borrowers with a more comprehensive understanding of the financial implications of their mortgage, as it takes into account not only the interest rate but also closing costs, points, mortgage insurance, and other expenses incurred during the loan process. By comparing APRs from different lenders, borrowers can evaluate the overall affordability and competitiveness of mortgage offers more accurately. A lower APR indicates a more favorable loan offer with lower total costs over the life of the loan, while a higher APR suggests higher borrowing costs. Therefore, understanding and comparing APRs is essential for homebuyers to make informed decisions when selecting a mortgage lender and loan product in the real estate market.

Adjustable-Rate Mortgage (ARM): An ARM is a type of mortgage loan where the interest rate can change periodically over the life of the loan. Typically, an ARM will have an initial fixed-rate period, during which the interest rate remains constant. This initial period can vary but is often set for a period of five, seven, or ten years. After the initial period, the interest rate may adjust annually or semi-annually, depending on the terms of the loan. When the interest rate adjusts, the borrower's monthly payment may increase or decrease, depending on whether the new rate is higher or lower than the initial rate. There are usually caps in place to limit how much the interest rate can increase or decrease in a given adjustment period, as well as over the life of the loan. ARMs can be attractive to borrowers who expect their income to increase in the future or who plan to sell the property before the initial fixed-rate period ends. However, they also carry the risk of payment increases if interest rates rise, which can make budgeting more challenging for borrowers. As such, borrowers considering an ARM should carefully consider their financial situation and ability to manage potential payment fluctuations.

Appreciation: The increase in the value of a property over time. This appreciation can result from various factors, including economic growth, inflation, market demand, and property improvements. For rental property investors, appreciation represents a significant source of wealth accumulation and ROI. As property values increase, investors can build equity and potentially realize substantial profits upon selling or refinancing their properties. Moreover, appreciation enhances the overall ROI, complementing rental income and other cash flow sources. Savvy investors often target properties in areas with strong economic fundamentals and growth potential to capitalize on appreciation opportunities. However, it's essential to recognize that appreciation is not guaranteed and can be influenced by market fluctuations and other external factors. Therefore, prudent investors conduct thorough market research and due diligence to assess the appreciation potential of rental properties as part of their investment strategy. Overall, appreciation plays a vital role in rental property investing, offering investors the opportunity to build long-term wealth and financial stability.

Assess: A comprehensive evaluation of various factors to determine the suitability of a rental property for generating profitable returns. This assessment encompasses both quantitative and qualitative aspects, including the property's location, market dynamics, potential rental income, expenses, and overall investment risk. Location plays a crucial role, as properties situated in desirable neighborhoods with strong rental demand tend to command higher rents and appreciate more consistently over time. Market analysis involves examining trends in rental rates, vacancy rates, job growth, and economic indicators to gauge the viability of rental income and property appreciation. Evaluating potential rental income involves estimating the achievable rent based on comparable properties, rental market conditions, and the property's condition and amenities. Conversely, assessing expenses involves forecasting maintenance costs, property taxes, insurance, property management fees, and other operational expenses to determine the property's NOI and cash flow potential. Moreover, assessing investment risk entails considering factors such as tenant turnover, regulatory changes, economic volatility, and potential capital expenditures to ensure the investment aligns with the investor's risk tolerance and financial goals. Overall, a thorough assessment of rental property investments is essential for making informed decisions and maximizing long-term returns.

Assessed Value: The value assigned to a property by a government assessor for the purpose of determining property taxes. This value is typically based on various factors such as the property's size, location, age, and condition. While assessed value is used primarily for tax purposes, it can also indirectly impact rental property investors. A property with a higher assessed value may incur higher property taxes, thereby reducing the net income generated by rental operations. Consequently, rental property investors often consider the assessed value when evaluating the overall financial performance and potential profitability of a property. However, it's important to note that assessed value does not always reflect the market value of a property accurately. Market conditions, property improvements, and other factors may result in discrepancies between assessed value and actual market value. Despite this, assessed value remains an essential consideration for rental property investors as part of their comprehensive financial analysis and management strategy.

B

Balloon Payment: A balloon payment in rental property investing is a large, lump-sum payment due at the end of a loan term, often associated with short-term mortgages or commercial property loans. This type of payment structure typically involves lower monthly payments during the loan period, making it attractive for investors looking to maximize cash flow in the initial years of property ownership. However, the balloon payment represents a significant financial obligation that must be planned for, as it usually requires refinancing, selling the property, or having sufficient cash reserves to cover the payment when it comes due. Investors might opt for loans with balloon payments if they anticipate an increase in the property's value or their income, enabling them to handle the large final payment more easily. While balloon payments can provide short-term financial flexibility, they also carry risks, especially if property values decline or financing conditions become less favorable. Properly managing this risk involves careful financial planning and a clear exit strategy to ensure that the investor can meet the balloon payment without jeopardizing their investment. Understanding the terms and implications of balloon payments is essential for making informed decisions in rental property investing.

Broker: A broker is a licensed professional who has undergone additional training beyond that of a real estate agent and has met the requirements to obtain a broker's license. Brokers can work independently or manage a real estate brokerage firm where they may supervise other agents. Brokers typically facilitate real estate transactions between buyers and sellers, landlords and tenants, or investors and developers. They have a deep understanding of the local real estate market and can provide guidance and assistance throughout the buying, selling, or renting process. Brokers may represent clients as either a seller's agent, buyer's agent, landlord's agent, or tenant's agent, depending on their specific needs and preferences. They act as intermediaries, negotiating on behalf of their clients to achieve the best possible outcomes. A broker typically offers advice on various aspects of real estate, including pricing, marketing, financing, legal issues, and property management. They stay informed about market trends, property values, zoning regulations, and other factors that can affect real estate transactions. Brokers who own or manage a brokerage firm are responsible for overseeing the day-to-day operations of the business, including hiring and training agents, maintaining compliance with licensing and regulatory requirements, managing finances, and marketing the brokerage's services. Brokers must adhere to strict ethical standards and comply with applicable real estate laws and regulations. They have a fiduciary duty to act in their clients' best interests and to maintain confidentiality and honesty throughout the transaction process.

Broker Opinion of Value (BOV): A professional estimate of a property's market worth provided by a licensed real estate broker or agent. In rental property investing, a BOV plays a crucial role in decision-making, offering insights into a property's current market value based on comparable sales, income potential, and prevailing market conditions. Brokers assess various factors, including property condition, location, rental income potential, and comparable rental rates, to derive a comprehensive valuation. Investors rely on BOVs to make informed decisions about purchasing, refinancing, or selling rental properties, ensuring they are well-positioned in the market and can optimize their investment strategies based on current property values and market trends.

Buyer's Agent: A licensed professional who works on behalf of individuals or entities looking to purchase real estate. They specialize in understanding the local market, identifying suitable properties, negotiating favorable terms, and guiding buyers through the purchase process. A crucial aspect of their role is to advocate for the buyer's best interests, aiming to secure the most advantageous deal possible. Buyer's agents possess in-depth knowledge of property values, trends, and potential pitfalls, offering invaluable insights to their clients. They typically start by understanding the buyer's needs, preferences, and budget constraints, tailoring their search accordingly. Throughout the property search, they conduct thorough due diligence, inspecting properties, analyzing market data, and advising on potential risks and rewards. During negotiations, buyer's agents leverage their expertise to secure favorable terms, including price, contingencies, and closing timelines. Their ultimate goal is to ensure that buyers make well-informed decisions and achieve their investment objectives in the real estate market.

Buyer's Market: A buyer's market refers to a market condition where there are more properties available for sale than there are interested buyers. This scenario typically results in decreased property prices, longer listing times, and increased competition among sellers. In a buyer's market, investors have the upper hand as they have more options to choose from and can negotiate better deals with motivated sellers looking to offload their properties. For rental property investors, a buyer's market presents an opportunity to snag properties at lower prices, negotiate favorable terms, and potentially secure higher rental yields due to the reduced acquisition costs. It is important for investors to conduct thorough market research and due diligence during a buyer's market to identify potentially lucrative investment opportunities and capitalize on the advantageous conditions prevalent in the real estate market.

C

Capitalization (CAP) Rate: CAP rate, short for capitalization rate, is a key metric used to evaluate the potential return on an investment property. The CAP rate is expressed as a percentage and is calculated by dividing the property's NOI by its current market value or purchase price. The CAP rate provides investors with a simple way to compare the ROI of different properties, regardless of their purchase price or financing terms. A higher CAP rate indicates a higher potential return relative to the property's value, while a lower CAP rate indicates a lower potential return. CAP rate is most useful when comparing similar properties within the same market or asset class. It provides a standardized metric for evaluating investment opportunities and making informed decisions about property acquisitions or portfolio management. Overall, CAP rate is a fundamental concept in real estate investment analysis and can help investors assess the income-generating potential of investment properties and make informed decisions about their investment strategy.

Capital: The financial resources required to acquire, maintain, and profitably operate real estate assets intended for rental income generation. This capital encompasses various components, including the initial purchase price of the property, closing costs, any necessary renovations or repairs to enhance rental appeal or property value, ongoing maintenance expenses, property taxes, insurance premiums, and contingency funds for unforeseen expenses. Additionally, investors may allocate capital for marketing efforts to attract tenants, property management fees if outsourcing management tasks, and reserves for vacancies or economic downturns. Effective capital management is paramount in rental property investing, as it ensures the property remains financially viable and can withstand fluctuations in the real estate market or unexpected expenses. Moreover, strategic allocation of capital allows investors to optimize returns, whether through regular rental income streams, property appreciation over time, or potential tax benefits associated with real estate investment. Ultimately, prudent management of capital is instrumental in building a resilient and profitable rental property portfolio.

Capital Expenditures (CAPEX): Capital Expenditures play a pivotal role in ensuring the long-term viability and profitability of your investment. CAPEX refers to the significant expenses incurred for the acquisition, improvement, or maintenance of a rental property that is expected to generate benefits over multiple years. These expenditures encompass a wide array of items, including but not limited to, major renovations, structural repairs, HVAC system replacements, roofing, and other upgrades that enhance the property's value or extend its lifespan. While CAPEX may seem daunting due to its upfront costs, prudent investors recognize its importance in preserving the property's appeal, functionality, and ultimately, its rental income potential. By strategically budgeting for CAPEX expenses, investors can mitigate the risk of unforeseen emergencies, prolong the property's lifespan, maintain tenant satisfaction, and ultimately maximize their ROI. Furthermore, diligent planning and proactive maintenance can help investors anticipate and manage CAPEX expenses effectively, thereby ensuring the continued success of their rental property endeavors.

Capital Gain: In rental property investing, capital gain refers to the profit realized from the sale of a rental property when the selling price exceeds the original purchase price plus any expenses incurred during acquisition and ownership. This financial gain is a critical aspect of real estate investing, as it directly impacts the investor's return on investment (ROI). When investors purchase a rental property, they often do so with the expectation that the property will appreciate in value over time due to factors such as market demand, improvements made to the property, and overall economic conditions. Capital gains can be short-term or long-term, depending on the holding period of the property, with long-term capital gains typically benefiting from favorable tax treatment. In many jurisdictions, long-term capital gains are taxed at a lower rate than ordinary income, making real estate a potentially lucrative investment option.

However, investors must also be aware of capital gains taxes, which can significantly impact the net profit from the sale. Strategies such as 1031 exchanges in the United States, where the proceeds from the sale are reinvested in a similar property to defer taxes, can help maximize the benefits of capital gains in rental property investing. Understanding and strategically managing capital gains is essential for investors seeking to optimize their real estate portfolio and achieve financial growth.

Cash Flow: A fundamental metric that measures the net income generated from rental operations after deducting all expenses. It represents the amount of money that flows in and out of the investment property on a regular basis. Positive cash flow occurs when rental income exceeds operating expenses, including mortgage payments, property taxes, insurance, maintenance, and vacancy costs. Positive cash flow is highly desirable for rental property investors as it provides a steady stream of income and enhances the property's overall ROI. It can be used to cover expenses, finance property improvements, build reserves for future repairs, or reinvest in additional rental properties. Conversely, negative cash flow occurs when expenses exceed rental income, resulting in a financial loss for the investor. While negative cash flow may be sustainable in the short term for strategic reasons such as property appreciation or tax benefits, it is generally considered less desirable and can strain the investor's financial resources. Therefore, prudent investors carefully analyze and manage cash flow to ensure the profitability and sustainability of their rental property investments over the long term.

Cash-out Refinance: A cash-out refinance is a financial strategy used by property owners to tap into the equity of a property by refinancing the existing mortgage with a new one that has a higher principal balance. In a cash-out refinance, the property owner borrows more than the remaining balance on the current mortgage, allowing them to receive a lump sum of cash from the equity built up in the property. The property owner can use the cash for various purposes, such as funding renovations, paying off high-interest debt, investing in additional properties, or covering personal expenses. The new mortgage obtained through the cash-out refinance will have updated terms, including a new interest rate, loan term, and monthly payment amount. It's essential for property owners to consider the impact of these changes on their overall financial situation and rental property cash flow.

Closing: A real estate closing, also known as settlement or escrow, is the final step in the process of transferring ownership of a property from the seller to the buyer. It is the culmination of all the negotiations, inspections, and paperwork involved in a real estate transaction. At the end of the closing, the parties receive a closing statement, also known as a settlement statement or HUD-1 form, which outlines all the financial transactions related to the sale. Once the closing process is complete, the buyer takes possession of the property, and the seller vacates the premises. The closing is a significant milestone in the real estate transaction, marking the official transfer of ownership and the completion of the sale.

Closing Costs: Closing Costs in rental property investing refer to the various fees and expenses incurred when finalizing the purchase of a property. These costs typically include lender fees, such as origination and underwriting fees, which are charged by the mortgage company for processing the loan. Additionally, there are appraisal and inspection fees to assess the property's value and condition, ensuring it meets the lender's and buyer's standards. Title insurance and title search fees protect against potential legal disputes over property ownership. Recording fees are paid to local government entities for documenting the sale. Prepaid expenses, such as property taxes, homeowners insurance, and interest, are also included, covering the period from closing to the first mortgage payment. Moreover, attorney fees may be required for legal services related to the transaction. These closing costs can significantly impact the initial outlay in rental property investing, often amounting to 2-5% of the property's purchase price, thus requiring careful financial planning and consideration.

Understanding and anticipating these expenses is crucial for investors to accurately assess the total investment needed and to ensure a profitable venture.

Closing Disclosure (CD): A CD is a standard form used in real estate transactions in the United States. It was introduced in October 2015 as part of the Consumer Financial Protection Bureau's (CFPB) 'Know Before You Owe' initiative, which aimed to simplify and improve the mortgage loan disclosure process. A CD is provided to borrowers by mortgage lenders at least three business days before the scheduled closing date of a mortgage loan. It serves as a detailed summary of the final terms and costs associated with the loan, allowing borrowers to review and compare the information with the Loan Estimate they received earlier in the process. Key components of a CD include loan terms, projected payments, closing costs, loan costs, loan calculations, etc. A CD is designed to provide borrowers with transparent and accurate information about the terms and costs of their mortgage loan before they finalize the transaction. It helps borrowers ensure that there are no surprises at the closing table and that they fully understand the financial implications of the loan.

Commission: The term commission refers to the fee paid to real estate agents or brokers for their services in facilitating a real estate transaction. When a property is sold, the seller typically pays a commission to their listing agent, who then splits the commission with the buyer's agent, if there is one involved in the transaction. The commission payments are typically made at the closing of the real estate transaction. The seller's proceeds from the sale are reduced by the amount of the commission, which is then distributed to the listing agent and cooperating broker. Real estate commissions are usually based on a percentage of the final sale price of the property, although they can also be structured as flat fees or a combination of both. The exact percentage or fee structure may vary depending on factors such as the local market norms, the complexity of the transaction, and the services provided by the real estate agents involved.

Condominium: A condominium, commonly referred to as a condo, is a type of residential real estate where a specified part of a larger property, typically an apartment-style unit, is individually owned. In addition to the individual units, condominiums also include shared common areas and amenities such as hallways, elevators, swimming pools, and recreational facilities, which are collectively owned and maintained by a HOA. Condo owners have title to their individual units and have shared ownership rights to the common areas. This shared ownership structure means that condo owners are required to pay monthly fees to the HOA to cover maintenance costs and other shared expenses. Condominiums offer a balance between owning a single-family home and renting an apartment, providing homeowners with the benefits of ownership while also offering shared amenities and community living.

Contingency: A contingency refers to a condition or requirement that must be met for a real estate contract to be binding. Contingencies protect buyers by allowing them to withdraw from a purchase contract without penalty if certain conditions are not met. Some common types of contingencies in real estate transactions are financing contingency, appraisal contingency, home inspection contingency, sale contingency, title contingency, etc. Contingencies are typically included in the purchase contract and must be satisfied or waived within a specified timeframe agreed upon by both parties. Failure to meet the contingency requirements within the designated timeframe may result in the termination of the contract, and the earnest money deposit may be refunded to the buyer. Contingencies provide important protections for buyers and help mitigate risks associated with real estate transactions.

Counteroffer: A pivotal juncture in negotiations between a buyer and a seller. When presented with an initial offer from the buyer, the seller may choose to respond with a counteroffer, proposing amendments or adjustments to the terms and conditions outlined in the original offer. This strategic move allows the seller to express their preferences, whether related to price, contingencies, closing timeline, or other aspects of the transaction. Similarly, buyers can also counter the seller's counteroffer, initiating a back-and-forth negotiation process aimed at reaching a mutually acceptable agreement. Counter-offers serve as a means for both parties to assert their interests while striving to strike a balance that maximizes their respective benefits. Effective negotiation skills, market knowledge, and a clear understanding of one's investment objectives are essential in navigating the counteroffer stage successfully. Ultimately, the outcome of this negotiation phase significantly influences the final terms of the purchase agreement and the overall success of the rental investment property acquisition.

Crowdfunding: In rental property investing, crowdfunding has emerged as a transformative approach, democratizing access to real estate markets that were traditionally the domain of wealthy investors and large institutions. This method involves pooling capital from a large number of individual investors, each contributing a relatively small amount, to collectively fund the purchase, renovation, and management of rental properties. Crowdfunding platforms, leveraging sophisticated technology, offer a variety of investment opportunities, ranging from residential homes to commercial real estate, with detailed information on projected returns, risks, and property specifics. These platforms often provide extensive vetting and due diligence, reducing the barrier to entry and mitigating risks for novice investors. Furthermore, crowdfunding in rental property investing allows for diversification, enabling investors to spread their capital across multiple properties and locations, thereby reducing exposure to the volatility and risks associated with single-property investments. This model not only provides a passive income stream through rental yields but also offers potential capital appreciation over time, making real estate investment more accessible, flexible, and attractive to a broader audience.

D

Debt Service: The regular payment of principal and interest on a mortgage loan used to finance the acquisition or improvement of rental properties. This payment is typically made monthly and covers the repayment of the borrowed principal amount along with the interest charged by the lender. Debt service is a critical aspect of rental property investing as it directly impacts the property's cash flow and financial performance. Investors must carefully manage their debt service obligations to ensure that rental income is sufficient to cover mortgage payments, thereby avoiding default and potential foreclosure. Moreover, the ratio of debt service to rental income, known as the debt service coverage ratio (DSCR), is a key metric used by lenders to assess the property's ability to generate enough income to meet its debt obligations. A healthy DSCR indicates that the property's rental income is sufficient to cover its debt service, providing lenders and investors with confidence in the property's financial viability. Overall, prudent management of debt service is essential for rental property investors to maintain financial stability, maximize cash flow, and achieve long-term success in the real estate market.

Debt-to-income (DTI) Ratio: The DTI ratio serves as a critical financial metric used by lenders to assess the borrower's ability to manage monthly mortgage payments in relation to their gross monthly income. This ratio compares the borrower's total monthly debt obligations, including mortgage payments, credit card payments, auto loans, and other debt, to their gross monthly income before taxes. The DTI ratio provides lenders with valuable insights into the borrower's financial health, indicating their capacity to take on additional debt responsibly. Lenders typically prefer borrowers with lower DTI ratios, as it signifies a lower risk of default and greater ability to manage their financial obligations. A lower DTI ratio suggests that the borrower has more disposable income available to cover mortgage payments, reducing the likelihood of financial strain or default. Lenders often have maximum DTI ratio thresholds that they are willing to accept for different types of loans, with conventional mortgages typically requiring lower ratios than government-backed loans. Borrowers with higher DTI ratios may still qualify for financing but may face higher interest rates or additional requirements to mitigate risk. Therefore, understanding and managing the DTI ratio is crucial for borrowers seeking real estate financing, as it directly impacts their eligibility for loans and overall financial stability in homeownership.

Deed: A deed is a legal document that transfers ownership of a property from one party (the grantor or seller) to another party (the grantee or buyer). It is a crucial component of the transfer of real property rights and serves as evidence of the ownership interest in the property. There are different types of deeds used in real estate transactions, each with its own implications and level of protection for the grantee. Common types of deeds include warranty deeds, quitclaim deeds, and special warranty deeds. Some key elements of a deed include names of the parties involved in the transaction, including the grantor (seller) and the grantee (buyer), a legal description of the property being transferred such as the property's address, boundaries, lot number, and any other identifying details necessary to accurately identify the property. Deeds may also contain various covenants and warranties that provide assurances to the grantee regarding the grantor's ownership interest in the property and the validity of the transfer. Common types of covenants include the covenant of seisin (asserting that the grantor owns the property), the covenant of quiet enjoyment (guaranteeing the grantee's right to use and enjoy the property without interference), and the covenant against encumbrances (warranting that the property is free from liens or other encumbrances). A deed is usually signed by the grantor and may also require witnesses and notarization to validate the transfer of ownership. Once executed, the deed is typically recorded with the appropriate government office, such as the county recorder's office, to provide public notice of the change in ownership and establish a chain of title.

Depreciation: In the context of rental property investment, depreciation is a fundamental concept that plays a crucial role in financial planning and taxation. It refers to the gradual decrease in the value of the property over time due to wear and tear, aging, and obsolescence. For rental property investors, depreciation offers significant tax benefits. The IRS allows property owners to deduct a portion of the property's cost each year as a depreciation expense, even though real estate often appreciates in value over the long term. This deduction reduces taxable income, lowering the investor's overall tax liability. The depreciation deduction is typically calculated based on the property's useful life, which the IRS sets at 27.5 years for residential rental properties and 39 years for commercial properties. To claim depreciation, investors must accurately determine the property's cost basis, excluding land value, and file the appropriate tax forms. Properly managing depreciation can enhance the property's cash flow by reducing taxes owed, making it a valuable tool for maximizing returns on rental property investments.

Disclosure: A critical aspect of a real estate transaction, serving to provide the buyer with comprehensive information about the property's condition, history, and potential risks. Sellers are typically required by law to disclose any material facts or defects that could affect the property's value or pose a risk to occupants. These disclosures may cover a wide range of issues, including structural defects, environmental hazards, past renovations, zoning restrictions, pending litigation, or any other pertinent information that could impact the buyer's decision-making process. Additionally, sellers may provide disclosures related to the property's rental history, current tenants, lease agreements, and financial performance. For buyers, carefully reviewing these disclosures is essential for making informed investment decisions, assessing potential risks, and understanding the property's true value. Working with experienced real estate professionals and conducting thorough due diligence can help buyers navigate the disclosure process effectively, ensuring transparency and minimizing the likelihood of future disputes or liabilities associated with the rental investment property.

Down Payment: A down payment is a portion of the purchase price that the buyer pays upfront in cash or by certified funds at the time of closing. The down payment is typically made by the buyer as part of their contribution toward purchasing the property, while the remaining balance is financed through a mortgage loan from a lender. It is a crucial aspect of financing a rental property and plays a significant role in determining the terms of the investment and the overall financial feasibility. Typically, lenders require a down payment ranging from 20% to 25% of the property's purchase price for traditional mortgage loans. However, the exact amount may vary based on factors such as the investor's creditworthiness, the type of property, and the lender's requirements. A higher down payment often results in more favorable loan terms, including lower interest rates and monthly mortgage payments, and may also help investors secure financing more easily. Investors may use personal savings, funds from retirement accounts, proceeds from the sale of other properties, or gifts from family members to cover the down payment. Additionally, some investors explore alternative financing options, such as government-backed loans with lower down payment requirements or creative financing strategies like seller financing. Understanding the significance of the down payment and carefully planning its allocation are essential steps for rental property investors to effectively manage cash flow, maximize returns, and mitigate risks in their investment ventures.

Dual Agent: A dual agent in rental property investing refers to a real estate agent who represents both the buyer and the seller in a transaction, or in the case of renting, both the landlord and the tenant. This dual representation can offer several advantages but also comes with inherent conflicts of interest. On the positive side, a dual agent can streamline the communication process, potentially expediting the transaction and reducing misunderstandings, as they have a comprehensive understanding of both parties' needs and objectives. Additionally, it can sometimes lead to a more straightforward negotiation process since the agent can facilitate compromises directly. However, the major drawback lies in the potential conflict of interest, as the dual agent must balance the interests of both parties, which can be challenging when their goals diverge. Ethical concerns also arise, as it is difficult for the agent to provide full fiduciary duty and undivided loyalty to both sides simultaneously. To mitigate these issues, transparency and disclosure are crucial, ensuring that both parties are fully aware of the dual agency arrangement and consent to it. Some jurisdictions have strict regulations governing dual agency to protect the interests of both parties involved in the rental property transaction.

Due Diligence: A meticulous and multifaceted process designed to uncover potential risks and verify the viability of an investment. This involves an exhaustive examination of the property's physical, financial, legal, and market characteristics. A physical inspection assesses the condition of the building, identifying necessary repairs, maintenance issues, and compliance with local building codes. Financial analysis includes reviewing historical income and expense statements, understanding current cash flow, and projecting future earnings to ensure the property can meet financial goals. Legal due diligence verifies the clear title of the property, checks for existing liens or disputes, and examines lease agreements for enforceability and terms that protect the investor's interests. Market analysis is crucial, involving the study of local real estate trends, rental demand, occupancy rates, and neighborhood amenities to gauge the property's potential for appreciation and consistent rental income. By thoroughly investigating these aspects, investors can identify red flags, negotiate favorable purchase terms, and make informed decisions that align with their investment strategies and risk appetite.

E

Earnest Money: In a real estate transaction, earnest money, also known as a good faith deposit, is a sum of money provided by the buyer to the seller as a demonstration of their serious intent to purchase the property. Earnest money is typically included with the purchase offer and is held in escrow until the closing of the transaction. Earnest money provides the seller with some assurance that the buyer will follow through with the purchase and fulfill their obligations under the contract. If the buyer later backs out of the deal without a valid reason, the seller may be entitled to keep the earnest money as compensation for taking the property off the market and potential damages. The amount of earnest money required can vary depending on factors such as the local real estate market, the purchase price of the property, and the preferences of the seller. Typically, earnest money is around 1% to 3% of the purchase price, but it can be higher in competitive markets or for high-value properties. If the sale goes through as planned and the transaction closes, the earnest money is typically applied toward the buyer's down payment and closing costs. However, if the sale falls through due to a valid reason specified in the purchase contract, such as a failed inspection or financing contingency, the earnest money is typically refunded to the buyer. If the buyer backs out of the deal without a valid reason, the seller may be entitled to keep the earnest money as compensation for the time and effort expended.

Equated Monthly Installment (EMI): In rental property investing, EMI plays a crucial role in managing the financial aspects of property acquisition and investment returns. EMI refers to the fixed monthly payments made by an investor to repay the loan taken to purchase the rental property. This installment comprises both the principal amount and the interest, ensuring the loan is paid off over a specified period. The EMI amount is determined by factors such as the loan amount, interest rate, and loan tenure. For rental property investors, calculating an affordable EMI is essential to maintain positive cash flow and ensure that the rental income covers the monthly repayments, as well as other property-related expenses like maintenance, taxes, and insurance. A well-planned EMI structure can optimize the investor's leverage, enabling them to maximize returns while minimizing financial stress. Additionally, understanding the amortization schedule, which is how the EMI payments are divided between principal and interest over the loan tenure, helps investors strategize their finances better, plan for future investments, and make informed

Equity: Equity is the ownership interest or value that an individual or entity holds in a property. It represents the difference between the property's market value and any outstanding debts or liens against it. In essence, it is the portion of the property that the owner truly owns outright and is a measure of the property's net worth. Equity can increase over time through several mechanisms, including appreciation in property value, mortgage principal payments, and property improvements that enhance its worth. As rental property values appreciate and mortgage balances decrease, equity typically grows. Equity is a critical metric for investors as it directly impacts their net worth and financial leverage. It serves as a source of wealth accumulation and can be leveraged through techniques like refinancing or home equity loans to access cash for further investment or other financial needs. Additionally, equity provides a measure of security and stability for investors, acting as a buffer against market fluctuations and unforeseen expenses, while also offering potential avenues for wealth generation and financial flexibility in rental property portfolios.

Escrow: Escrow refers to a process where a neutral third party, known as an escrow agent or escrow holder, holds funds and documents on behalf of the buyer and seller until all conditions of the transaction have been met. Escrow serves as a safeguard for both parties by ensuring that the terms of the sale are fulfilled before the funds are disbursed and the title is transferred. When purchasing rental property, funds for the property purchase, such as the down payment and closing costs, are typically deposited into an escrow account managed by an escrow agent or company. This ensures that the funds are safely held until all conditions of the sale are met, including property inspections, title searches, and any other contingencies outlined in the purchase agreement. Once all requirements are satisfied, the escrow agent disburses the funds to the seller, and the property ownership is transferred to the buyer. Escrow provides a level of security and transparency for both parties involved, mitigating the risk of fraud or disputes during the transaction process. Additionally, escrow can also be used in rental agreements to hold security deposits, ensuring that funds are returned to tenants appropriately at the end of the lease term, subject to any deductions for damages or unpaid rent as outlined in the lease agreement.

Eviction: A critical and often challenging process that involves legally removing a tenant from a rental property due to violations of the lease agreement or non-payment of rent. This process is typically governed by local and state laws, which set forth specific procedures and timelines that landlords must follow to ensure the eviction is lawful. Initially, the landlord must provide the tenant with a formal notice, which varies based on the reason for eviction, such as a "pay or quit" notice for non-payment of rent or a "cure or quit" notice for lease violations. If the tenant fails to comply within the stipulated period, the landlord must then file an eviction lawsuit, known as an unlawful detainer, in court. The court process involves a hearing where both parties can present their case, and if the court rules in favor of the landlord, a judgment for possession is issued. Subsequently, the landlord can obtain a writ of possession, which authorizes law enforcement to physically remove the tenant if they do not leave voluntarily. Eviction can be costly and time-consuming, often involving legal fees and lost rental income, and can also lead to property damage and strained landlord-tenant relationships. Therefore, landlords are encouraged to conduct thorough tenant screening to minimize the risk of eviction and to explore alternative dispute-resolution methods before resorting to legal action.

Exclusive Listing: A contractual agreement between a property owner and a single real estate agent or brokerage, granting the latter the sole right to market and sell the property for a specified period. This exclusive arrangement means that the agent has the exclusive authority to advertise the property, conduct showings, negotiate with potential buyers, and ultimately facilitate the sale. The agent is typically more motivated to invest significant resources into marketing efforts, such as professional photography, staging, open houses, and targeted advertising campaigns, knowing that they are guaranteed a commission if the property sells within the exclusivity period. For property owners, this can result in more personalized service, focused marketing strategies, and potentially quicker sales, as the agent is dedicated to achieving the best possible outcome. Additionally, having a single point of contact streamlines communication and reduces the confusion that can arise from working with multiple agents. However, it is imperative for property owners to choose an experienced and reputable agent, as the success of the exclusive listing largely depends on the agent's capability to attract qualified buyers and effectively close the sale. If the agent underperforms, the property may linger on the market, potentially delaying the sale and impacting the owner's financial goals.

F

Fannie Mae: Fannie Mae, officially known as the Federal National Mortgage Association (FNMA), is a government-sponsored enterprise (GSE) established by the United States Congress in 1938. It was created to expand the secondary mortgage market by buying mortgages from lenders and then either holding those mortgages in its portfolio or packaging them into mortgage-backed securities (MBS) for sale to investors. Fannie Mae plays a significant role in the United States housing finance system by providing liquidity to the mortgage market. By purchasing mortgages from lenders, Fannie Mae helps to replenish lenders' funds so they can issue more mortgages to homebuyers. Their mission includes promoting homeownership by increasing access to mortgage credit for qualified borrowers. It achieves this by establishing underwriting standards, providing mortgage products with competitive terms, and supporting affordable housing initiatives. While Fannie Mae is a publicly traded company, it operates with a government charter and enjoys certain privileges, such as access to low-cost funding through the issuance of debt securities with implied government backing. However, it's important to note that Fannie Mae is not backed by the full faith and credit of the United States government. Fannie Mae is regulated by the Federal Housing Finance Agency (FHFA), which oversees its safety and soundness and ensures that it fulfills its public mission while operating in a safe and prudent manner.

FHA Loan: An FHA loan is a mortgage loan insured by the FHA, which is part of the United States Department of HUD. These loans are designed to make homeownership more accessible, particularly for first-time homebuyers and those with lower credit scores or limited down payment funds. Key features of FHA loans include low down payment, flexible credit requirements, mortgage insurance, etc. FHA loans have specific property requirements, including minimum property standards that must be met for the home to be eligible for FHA financing. These loans are popular among borrowers who may not otherwise qualify for conventional financing due to factors such as low credit scores or limited down payment funds.

Final Walk-Through: A final walk-through is a crucial step before closing on a rental investment property. It typically occurs a few days before the closing date. During this process, the buyer walks through the property to ensure that it is in the same condition as when they agreed to purchase it and that any agreed-upon repairs or changes have been made. They check for any new damages or issues that may have arisen since the last inspection. If there were any repairs or changes agreed upon between the buyer and seller, the investor verifies that these have been completed satisfactorily. This could include repairs to appliances, plumbing, electrical systems, or any other agreed-upon work. The investor ensures that all inclusions specified in the purchase agreement are present in the property. The investor also checks that all utilities are working correctly and that essential systems such as heating, cooling, plumbing, and electrical are functioning properly. The final walk-through is essential for investors to make sure they are getting what they paid for and to address any last-minute concerns before completing the purchase. If any issues are identified during the walk-through, the investor can address them with the seller before the closing date.

Financing: In rental property investment, financing refers to the various methods investors use to fund the purchase of income-generating properties. Unlike purchasing a primary residence, where buyers typically secure a mortgage, rental property investors have several financing options tailored to their investment goals and financial situation. One common method is obtaining a traditional mortgage loan, where investors make a down payment (often around 20-25% of the property's purchase price) and finance the remaining amount through a lender. The rental income generated from tenants is often used to cover mortgage payments and expenses and to generate profit. Another financing avenue is through government-backed loans, such as those offered by the FHA or the Department of Veterans Affairs (VA), which may require lower down payments or offer more favorable terms. Investors also explore creative financing options like seller financing, where the property seller acts as the lender, allowing the buyer to make payments directly to them over time. Additionally, investors may consider partnerships, private money loans, or tapping into home equity through cash-out refinancing on existing properties to fund new purchases. Choosing the right financing strategy is critical for rental property investors to optimize cash flow, manage risk, and achieve their long-term investment objectives.

Fixed-Rate Mortgage: A Fixed-Rate Mortgage is a type of mortgage loan where the interest rate remains constant for the entire term of the loan. This means that the borrower's monthly principal and interest payments stay the same throughout the life of the loan, providing predictability and stability in budgeting. With a fixed-rate mortgage, the interest rate is determined at the time the loan is originated and does not change, regardless of fluctuations in the broader interest rate market. This makes fixed-rate mortgages popular among borrowers who prefer the security of knowing their mortgage payments will remain consistent over time, regardless of changes in the economy or financial markets. Fixed-rate mortgages are available with various term lengths, typically ranging from 10 to 30 years. Shorter-term loans generally have higher monthly payments but lower total interest costs over the life of the loan, while longer-term loans offer lower monthly payments but higher total interest costs. Overall, fixed-rate mortgages are well-suited for borrowers who plan to keep their property for an extended period or who prefer the stability of consistent payments over time.

Foreclosure: Foreclosure refers to the legal process by which a lender takes possession of a property from a borrower (typically the property owner) who has defaulted on their mortgage loan. Foreclosure occurs when the borrower fails to make timely payments on the loan, leading to a default and eventual loss of the property. Foreclosure is a serious and potentially devastating outcome for property owners, as it results in the loss of their property and may also have long-term financial and legal consequences. However, on occasion, there are options available to property owners facing foreclosure, such as loan modifications, forbearance, short sales, and deed in lieu of foreclosure arrangements, which may provide alternatives to foreclosure and mitigate the impact on the borrower.

Freddie Mac: Freddie Mac, officially known as the Federal Home Loan Mortgage Corporation (FHLMC), is a GSE established by Congress in 1970. Similar to Fannie Mae, Freddie Mac was created to expand the secondary mortgage market and increase access to affordable mortgage credit for homebuyers. Freddie Mac operates in the secondary mortgage market, purchasing mortgages from lenders and packaging them into MBS for sale to investors. This process helps to replenish lenders' funds so they can issue more mortgages to borrowers. Like Fannie Mae, Freddie Mac's mission includes promoting homeownership by providing liquidity to the mortgage market and supporting access to mortgage credit for qualified borrowers. It offers a range of mortgage products with competitive terms to help borrowers finance their homes and is regulated by the FHFA, which oversees its safety and soundness and ensures that it fulfills its public mission while operating in a safe and prudent manner. Fannie Mae tends to buy loans from larger commercial banks and lenders whereas Freddie Mac usually buys loans from smaller banks or credit unions. This is the primary difference between the two. Fannie Mae has also been around about 30 years longer than Freddie Mac.

FSBO (For Sale By Owner): FSBO, which stands for 'For Sale By Owner,' is a term used in real estate to describe a property that is being sold directly by the owner without the assistance of a real estate agent or broker. In an FSBO transaction, the owner takes on the responsibilities traditionally handled by a real estate agent, including marketing the property, negotiating with potential buyers, and completing the sale process. FSBO transactions can offer potential benefits for sellers, such as greater control over the sales process and savings on commission fees. However, they also require sellers to invest time, effort, and resources into effectively marketing and selling their property and navigating the complexities of the real estate transaction process without professional representation. As such, FSBO may not be suitable for all sellers and properties, and some may prefer to work with a real estate agent for guidance and support throughout the sale process.

G

Good Faith Estimate (GFE): The GFE was a standard form used in real estate transactions in the United States until October 2015. It was required by the Real Estate Settlement Procedures Act (RESPA), a federal law that aimed to ensure transparency and fairness in mortgage transactions. The GFE was provided by mortgage lenders to borrowers within three days of applying for a mortgage loan. It outlined the estimated costs and fees associated with obtaining a mortgage, including origination charges, title charges, settlement charges, prepaid items, etc. The purpose of the GFE was to help borrowers understand the total costs involved in obtaining a mortgage loan and to compare offers from different lenders more easily. It was an important tool for promoting transparency and preventing hidden fees or predatory lending practices. In October 2015, the GFE was replaced by two new forms: the Loan Estimate (LE) and the Closing Disclosure (CD).

Grant Deed: A Grant Deed is a legal document commonly used in real estate transactions to transfer ownership of real property from one party to another. This document contains crucial information such as the names of the current owner (grantor) and the new owner (grantee), a legal description of the property being transferred, and any conditions or restrictions associated with the transfer. Unlike a Quitclaim Deed, which only transfers the interest the grantor may have in the property without any guarantees, a Grant Deed guarantees that the grantor has the legal right to transfer the property and that the property is free from any undisclosed encumbrances, except for those specifically noted in the deed. Grant Deeds are typically recorded with the county recorder's office to provide a public record of the transfer, ensuring that the new owner's rights to the property are legally recognized and protected. This document serves as essential evidence of ownership in real estate transactions and helps establish clear title to the property.

Gross Income Multiplier (GIM): The GIM is a significant metric used in real estate investment analysis to evaluate the value of income-producing properties. It is calculated by dividing the property's sale price by its gross annual rental income. This ratio provides investors with a quick and simplified way to assess the property's potential ROI based on its income generation. A lower GIM typically indicates a better investment opportunity, as it suggests that the property is priced lower relative to its income potential. However, it's essential to consider other factors such as operating expenses, vacancy rates, and market trends alongside the GIM to make a comprehensive assessment of the property's investment viability. Despite its simplicity, the GIM is a valuable tool for real estate investors to quickly compare different properties and identify potential opportunities for further analysis and consideration.

Gross Rental Income: The total amount of revenue generated from renting out a property before deducting any expenses. It includes all income received from tenants, such as monthly rent payments, pet fees, parking fees, and any other rental-related income. Gross rental income is a crucial metric for rental property investors as it directly impacts the property's financial performance and profitability. It provides investors with an indication of the property's earning potential and serves as the foundation for assessing its cash flow and ROI. Maximizing gross rental income is often a primary objective for investors, achieved through strategic pricing strategies, effective property management, and maintaining high occupancy rates. However, it's important to note that gross rental income does not reflect the property's true profitability since it does not account for expenses such as property taxes, insurance, maintenance, vacancies, and property management fees. Therefore, while gross rental income provides valuable insights into the revenue-generating capacity of a rental property, investors must analyze it in conjunction with operating expenses to evaluate the property's overall financial performance accurately.

H

Home Inspection: A home inspection is a critical step in the process of buying or selling a property in real estate. Conducted by a licensed and experienced home inspector, this thorough examination assesses the condition of a home's structural components, systems, and overall functionality. Home inspections typically cover aspects such as the foundation, roof, plumbing, electrical systems, HVAC systems, insulation, and the condition of appliances. The inspection report provides detailed information about any existing issues, safety concerns, or potential problems that may require attention or repairs. For buyers, a home inspection helps uncover any hidden defects or deficiencies in the property, allowing them to make informed decisions and negotiate repairs or adjustments to the purchase price. Sellers benefit from home inspections by identifying and addressing issues upfront, potentially increasing the marketability and value of their property. Overall, home inspections play a vital role in ensuring transparency, protecting both buyers and sellers, and facilitating smoother real estate transactions.

Homeowners Association (HOA): An HOA is a private organization established within a residential community, typically consisting of homeowners within that community. The primary purpose of an HOA is to manage and maintain common areas, amenities, and shared facilities within the community, such as parks, swimming pools, roads, and landscaping. Homeowners are usually required to pay regular dues or assessments to the HOA, which are used to fund these maintenance activities and other community services. Additionally,

HOAs often enforce rules and regulations known as CC&Rs (Covenants, Conditions, and Restrictions) that govern various aspects of property ownership and behavior within the community. These rules may cover issues such as architectural guidelines, landscaping standards, noise restrictions, and pet policies. While HOAs can provide valuable benefits such as enhanced property values and community amenities, they also come with potential drawbacks, including additional costs, restrictions on property use, and potential conflicts with neighbors or the HOA board. Therefore, it's essential for homebuyers to carefully review the HOA's rules, financial status, and governing documents before purchasing a property within an HOA-managed community.

HUD-1 Settlement Statement: The HUD-1 Settlement Statement is a standardized form used in real estate transactions in the United States, especially for residential purchases involving federally regulated mortgage loans. It outlines all financial transactions and disbursements involved in the closing of a real estate sale, providing a detailed breakdown of costs and credits for both the buyer and seller. The form is named after the Department of Housing and Urban Development (HUD), which oversees its use. The HUD-1 Settlement Statement includes information such as the purchase price, loan fees, prorated property taxes, insurance premiums, and any other expenses related to the transaction. It serves as a vital document for ensuring transparency and accuracy in the closing process, allowing all parties involved to review and verify the final financial details of the sale. Additionally, the HUD-1 Settlement Statement is often required by lenders, title companies, and regulatory authorities as part of the documentation for mortgage loans and real estate transactions.

I

Inspection: A crucial step in the due diligence process, allowing buyers to thoroughly evaluate the condition of the property before finalizing the transaction. These inspections are typically conducted by qualified professionals, such as licensed home inspectors, who assess various aspects of the property, including its structural integrity, mechanical systems, electrical wiring, plumbing, roofing, and overall safety compliance. Through detailed inspections, buyers can uncover hidden defects, potential safety hazards, or maintenance issues that may impact the property's value or require immediate attention. The inspection report provides buyers with valuable insights into the property's current condition, allowing them to make informed decisions about the purchase and negotiate repairs or concessions with the seller as needed. Additionally, inspections provide an opportunity for buyers to gain a deeper understanding of the property's maintenance requirements and projected expenses, helping them formulate a realistic budget and investment strategy. By prioritizing thorough inspections, buyers can mitigate risks, safeguard their investment, and ensure the long-term profitability of their rental property venture.

Inspection Contingency: An inspection contingency is a provision included in a purchase agreement that allows the buyer a specified period, typically ranging from a few days to a week or more, to conduct inspections on the property. These inspections may include examinations of the property's structural integrity, mechanical systems, plumbing, electrical systems, roofing, and any other aspects that may affect its value or habitability. The purpose of the inspection contingency is to give the buyer the opportunity to thoroughly evaluate the property's condition and identify any issues or defects that may not be immediately apparent. If significant issues are uncovered during the inspection period, the buyer can negotiate with the seller to address the problems, either through repairs, credits, or a reduction in the purchase price. In some cases, buyers may choose to withdraw from the transaction entirely if the inspection reveals major concerns that cannot be resolved satisfactorily. The inspection contingency provides buyers with a crucial level of protection and allows them to make more informed decisions about the purchase, ensuring that they are not caught unaware by unforeseen problems after closing.

Interest Rate: Interest rate in real estate refers to the percentage of the loan amount that a lender charges a borrower for the use of their money, typically expressed as an APR. In real estate transactions, interest rates play a significant role in determining the cost of borrowing funds to purchase a property. These rates are influenced by various factors, including economic conditions, inflation, central bank policies, and the borrower's creditworthiness. Lower interest rates generally make borrowing more affordable, stimulating demand for real estate purchases and potentially increasing property values. Conversely, higher interest rates can reduce affordability, leading to decreased demand and potentially lower property prices. For homebuyers, securing a favorable interest rate is crucial as it directly impacts the monthly mortgage payments and the overall cost of homeownership over the life of the loan. Real estate investors also closely monitor interest rates, as they affect the profitability of investment properties and the feasibility of financing strategies. Therefore, understanding and staying informed about interest rate trends is essential for all parties involved in real estate transactions.

Investor: A real estate investor is an individual or entity that allocates capital with the goal of generating a return through the acquisition, ownership, management, or sale of real property. Real estate investors can pursue various strategies, including rental property ownership, property development, REITs, flipping properties for profit, or investing in real estate-related securities. These investors analyze market trends, property values, rental income potential, and economic indicators to identify opportunities for investment. They often leverage financing options such as mortgages, private loans, or partnerships to acquire properties and maximize returns on investment. Real estate investors aim to generate income through rental payments, appreciation in property values, or both. Additionally, they manage risks associated with property ownership, such as vacancies, property maintenance, market volatility, and regulatory changes. Successful real estate investors employ sound financial strategies, conduct thorough due diligence, and adapt their investment approaches to market conditions to achieve their investment objectives in the dynamic real estate market.

IRS (Internal Revenue Service): The federal agency responsible for administering and enforcing the tax laws of the United States. It operates under the authority of the Department of the Treasury and is tasked with collecting taxes, processing tax returns, and ensuring compliance with tax laws. Investors can leverage several IRS provisions to minimize their taxable income, such as depreciation, which allows the cost of the property (excluding land) to be deducted over a period of 27.5 years for residential rental properties. This non-cash deduction can reduce taxable income, thereby increasing overall cash flow. Additionally, the IRS permits the deduction of mortgage interest, property taxes, insurance, and maintenance expenses, further decreasing the taxable rental income. The 1031 Exchange is another critical IRS-sanctioned benefit, allowing investors to defer capital gains taxes by reinvesting proceeds from the sale of one property into a like-kind property. This deferral strategy facilitates portfolio growth and wealth accumulation without immediate tax liabilities. Moreover, investors can utilize the home office deduction if they manage their rental properties from a dedicated space within their home, allowing a portion of their home expenses to be deducted. These tax benefits, when properly managed and documented, can lead to substantial financial advantages, making rental property investing a lucrative endeavor under the guidelines set by the IRS.

J

Joint Tenancy: Joint tenancy is a form of property ownership where two or more individuals, often referred to as joint tenants, hold equal and undivided interests in a property. One of the defining features of joint tenancy is the right of survivorship, which means that if one joint tenant dies, their ownership interest automatically transfers to the surviving joint tenant(s) without the need for probate. This aspect distinguishes joint tenancy from other forms of co-ownership, such as tenancy in common, where each owner's share can be passed on to heirs through a will or intestate succession. Joint tenancy is commonly used by married couples, family members, or business partners who want to ensure that ownership of the property seamlessly transfers to the surviving owner(s) upon death. To create a joint tenancy, the co-owners must acquire the property at the same time, through the same deed, and with equal ownership interests. Additionally, joint tenants must have unity of time, title, interest, and possession, as well as the right to use and enjoy the entire property. While joint tenancy offers benefits such as simplified transfer of ownership and protection against probate, it also requires trust and cooperation among the co-owners, as any joint tenant can unilaterally sever the joint tenancy, converting it into a tenancy in common, by transferring their interest to another party.

Jumbo Loan: A jumbo loan refers to a type of mortgage loan that exceeds the conforming loan limits set by GSEs like Fannie Mae and Freddie Mac. These limits are established to regulate the size of loans that these agencies can guarantee or purchase on the secondary mortgage market. Since jumbo loans exceed these limits, they typically cannot be purchased or securitized by Fannie Mae or Freddie Mac and are considered non-conforming loans. As a result, jumbo loans often carry higher interest rates and stricter qualification requirements compared to conforming loans. Jumbo loans are commonly used to finance high-end or luxury properties, as well as properties in expensive real estate markets where home prices exceed the conforming loan limits. Borrowers seeking jumbo loans usually need strong credit scores, low DTI ratios, and substantial down payments to qualify. Lenders may also require additional documentation and reserves to mitigate the higher risk associated with jumbo loans. Despite the higher costs and stricter requirements, jumbo loans provide an essential financing option for buyers looking to purchase higher-priced properties beyond the limits of conforming loans.

K

Keybox: A keybox or lockbox is a secure container typically attached to the doorknob or another fixed object near the entrance of a property. It is used to store keys to the property and allows authorized individuals, such as real estate agents and potential buyers, to access the property for showings and inspections when the owner is not present. Overall, lockboxes are a practical tool used in real estate to facilitate property showings and access for authorized individuals while maintaining security and control over property keys. They play a crucial role in streamlining the showing process and maximizing exposure for listed properties, ultimately helping sellers attract potential buyers and expedite the sale process.

Kickback: A kickback refers to a situation where a real estate professional, such as a real estate agent or broker, receives a payment or some other form of compensation from a third party in exchange for referring clients or customers to them. This practice can occur in various forms, including cash payments, gifts, or services rendered. Kickbacks can potentially compromise the integrity of the real estate transaction by influencing the agent's recommendation or decision-making process, as they may prioritize their own financial gain over the best interests of their clients. Such actions could violate ethical standards and even laws governing real estate transactions, leading to legal repercussions and damage to the agent's reputation. Therefore, it's essential for real estate professionals to adhere to strict ethical guidelines and regulations to maintain transparency and trust within the industry. Additionally, clients should be vigilant and cautious when engaging with real estate agents to ensure that their interests are being prioritized above any potential kickback arrangements.

L

Lease Agreement: A legally binding contract that outlines the terms and conditions between a landlord and a tenant for the rental of a property. It serves as a crucial document that establishes the rights and responsibilities of both parties throughout the duration of the tenancy. The lease agreement typically includes details such as the names of the landlord and tenant, the address and description of the rental property, the duration of the lease term (e.g., month-to-month, yearly), the amount of rent, the due date for rent payments, the security deposit amount and terms, rules regarding pets, smoking, and property maintenance responsibilities. Additionally, it may cover provisions for late payments, utilities, repairs, and procedures for resolving disputes. A well-crafted lease agreement helps to protect both the landlord and the tenant by clearly delineating their respective obligations and expectations, ultimately fostering a harmonious landlord-tenant relationship and providing a framework for resolving any issues that may arise during the tenancy.

Leasing Agent: A leasing agent, also known as a rental agent or rental broker, is a professional within the real estate industry who specializes in assisting individuals or businesses with finding and leasing rental properties. Their primary role is to act as intermediaries between landlords and tenants, helping both parties navigate the rental process efficiently and effectively. Rental agents possess in-depth knowledge of the local rental market, including current rental rates, available properties, and neighborhood amenities, allowing them to match tenants with suitable rental options based on their preferences and budget. They provide valuable guidance and assistance to tenants throughout the rental search process, from identifying potential properties and scheduling viewings to negotiating lease terms and completing rental applications. Additionally, rental agents often handle administrative tasks such as preparing lease agreements, conducting background and credit checks on prospective tenants, and coordinating move-in logistics. Their expertise and professionalism streamline the rental process for both landlords and tenants, ensuring a smooth and successful rental experience.

Leverage: The strategic use of borrowed funds, typically in the form of a mortgage loan, to increase the potential ROI. By leveraging borrowed capital, investors can amplify their purchasing power and acquire properties that they may not be able to afford solely with their own funds. Leverage works by allowing investors to use a smaller amount of their own money as a down payment while financing the remaining purchase price with a loan. This means that investors can control a more substantial asset with a relatively smaller investment, potentially magnifying their returns if the property appreciates in value. However, it's important to recognize that leverage also increases risk, as borrowing magnifies both gains and losses. Therefore, prudent investors carefully consider the risks associated with leverage, including interest rate fluctuations, market volatility, and potential cash flow constraints. Nevertheless, when used wisely, leverage can be a powerful tool for rental property investors to accelerate wealth accumulation, diversify their portfolios, and achieve long-term financial success in the real estate market.

Listing Agent: A listing agent, also known as a seller's agent, is a licensed real estate professional who represents the interests of the property seller in a real estate transaction. Their primary responsibility is to assist the seller in marketing and selling their property for the best possible price and terms. Listing agents typically provide a range of services, including conducting market research to determine the property's value, advising the seller on preparing the property for sale, creating and implementing a marketing plan to attract potential buyers, coordinating property showings and open houses, negotiating offers on behalf of the seller, and guiding the seller through the closing process. Additionally, listing agents serve as intermediaries between the seller and prospective buyers, facilitating communication and addressing any concerns or questions that may arise during the sales process. Their expertise in pricing strategies, market trends, and negotiation skills are invaluable assets to sellers, helping them achieve their goals and maximize their returns on the sale of their property. Listing Agreement: A contract between a property owner and a real estate agent or broker, authorizing them to market and sell the property.

Loan Estimate (LE): An LE is a standard form used in real estate transactions in the United States. It was introduced in October 2015 as part of the CFPB "Know Before You Owe" initiative, which aimed to simplify and improve the mortgage loan disclosure process. A LE provides borrowers with a detailed summary of the terms and estimated costs associated with a mortgage loan they have applied for. Mortgage lenders are required to provide a LE to borrowers within three business days of receiving a completed loan application. Key components of a LE include loan terms, projected payments, closing costs, loan costs, etc. A LE is designed to provide borrowers with clear and concise information about the terms and costs of their mortgage loan, enabling them to make informed decisions when comparing loan offers and understanding the total cost of property ownership.

Loan Modification: A vital financial tool in rental property investing, offering a lifeline for property owners facing difficulties in meeting their mortgage obligations. This process involves negotiating new terms with the lender to make the loan more manageable, often by reducing the interest rate, extending the loan term, or converting an ARM to a fixed-rate one. For rental property investors, a successful loan modification can significantly lower monthly mortgage payments, thus improving cash flow and financial stability. It can also prevent foreclosure, allowing investors to retain ownership of their properties and continue generating rental income. The process typically requires demonstrating financial hardship and the ability to adhere to the new loan terms, necessitating thorough documentation and communication with the lender. While the modification process can be complex and time-consuming, the benefits often outweigh the challenges, offering a strategic way to navigate financial difficulties and preserve long-term investment goals. By securing more favorable loan terms, investors can stabilize their portfolios, maintain tenant relations, and ultimately ensure the sustained profitability of their rental properties.

Loan Origination Fee: In real estate transactions involving mortgages, a loan origination fee is a charge imposed by a lender to cover the costs associated with processing and underwriting a loan. This fee is typically expressed as a percentage of the total loan amount and is paid by the borrower at the time of closing. The loan origination fee compensates the lender for the various services and expenses incurred during the loan origination process, including application processing, credit checks, property appraisals, and administrative overhead. While the specific amount of the origination fee can vary depending on the lender and the complexity of the loan, it generally ranges from 0.5% to 1% of the loan amount. The origination fee is disclosed to the borrower upfront as part of the LE provided by the lender, allowing borrowers to understand the total costs associated with obtaining the loan. It's important for borrowers to carefully review and compare origination fees from different lenders when shopping for a mortgage, as this fee can significantly impact the overall cost of borrowing.

Loan-to-Value (LTV) Ratio: In real estate financing, the LTV ratio is a critical metric used by lenders to assess the risk associated with a mortgage loan. It represents the ratio of the loan amount to the appraised value or purchase price of the property being financed. The LTV ratio provides lenders with an indication of the level of equity or down payment the borrower is putting into the property, which in turn helps them evaluate the likelihood of repayment and determine the terms of the loan, including interest rates and required mortgage insurance. A lower LTV ratio indicates that the borrower has more equity in the property, which typically translates to lower risk for the lender. Conversely, a higher LTV ratio suggests that the borrower has less equity and may pose a higher risk of default. Lenders often have maximum LTV ratios that they are willing to accept for different types of loans, with conventional mortgages typically requiring lower ratios than government-backed loans. Borrowers with higher LTV ratios may be subject to additional requirements such as private mortgage insurance (PMI) or higher interest rates to offset the increased risk to the lender. Understanding and managing the LTV ratio is crucial for borrowers seeking financing for real estate purchases, as it can have a significant impact on loan approval and terms.

Lockbox: A lockbox or keybox is a secure container typically attached to the doorknob or another fixed object near the entrance of a property. It is used to store keys to the property and allows authorized individuals, such as real estate agents and potential buyers, to access the property for showings and inspections when the owner is not present. Overall, lockboxes are a practical tool used in real estate to facilitate property showings and access for authorized individuals while maintaining security and control over property keys. They play a crucial role in streamlining the showing process and maximizing exposure for listed properties, ultimately helping sellers attract potential buyers and expedite the sale process.

M

Market Value: The estimated price at which a property would sell under current market conditions, assuming a willing buyer and seller. It represents the fair and objective assessment of a property's worth based on various factors such as location, size, condition, amenities, and recent comparable sales in the area. Understanding the market value of a rental property is essential for investors as it serves as a benchmark for determining the property's potential profitability and ROI. Investors use market value to assess whether a property is priced competitively relative to similar properties in the market and to make informed decisions about acquisition, disposition, or refinancing. Moreover, market value directly influences the property's financing options, appraisal, and insurance coverage. While market value provides valuable insights into a property's worth, it's important to recognize that it can fluctuate over time due to changes in market conditions, supply and demand dynamics, economic trends, and other factors. Therefore, savvy investors conduct thorough market research and analysis to accurately assess the market value of rental properties and make informed investment decisions that align with their financial goals and objectives.

Modified Accelerated Cost Recovery System (MACRS): A crucial tax provision utilized in rental property investing to optimize tax benefits and enhance cash flow. Implemented by the IRS, MACRS allows property investors to depreciate the value of their rental properties over a set period, effectively reducing their taxable income. For residential rental properties, MACRS assigns a recovery period of 27.5 years, during which investors can annually deduct a portion of the property's value (excluding land) from their taxable income. This depreciation is calculated using the declining balance method, which accelerates the depreciation rate in the earlier years of the property's life, providing higher deductions upfront. These larger initial deductions can be particularly beneficial for investors, as they help offset higher initial expenses and improve cash flow during the critical early stages of property ownership. By systematically depreciating the property, investors can reduce their overall tax liability, preserving more of their rental income and enhancing the property's profitability. Properly applying MACRS requires meticulous record keeping and adherence to IRS guidelines, but the resulting tax advantages make it a powerful tool in the financial strategy of rental property investors.

Mortgage: In investment real estate, mortgages play a pivotal role in leveraging capital to acquire income-generating properties. Investors often utilize mortgages as a means to finance the purchase of commercial or residential properties with the expectation of generating rental income or appreciation in property value. Unlike residential mortgages, which primarily focus on the borrower's ability to repay the loan based on personal income and creditworthiness, investment property mortgages primarily consider the income potential of the property itself. Lenders assess factors such as the property's rental income, operating expenses, potential vacancy rates, and overall cash flow to determine the loan amount and terms. By obtaining a mortgage, investors can acquire properties with a smaller initial cash outlay, allowing them to diversify their real estate portfolio and potentially increase returns on investment through property appreciation and rental income. However, investors must carefully consider the risks associated with leveraging debt, including interest rate fluctuations, potential vacancies, and market downturns, to ensure that the investment remains financially viable over the long term. Proper due diligence, financial analysis, and risk management are essential components of using mortgages effectively in investment real estate.

Mortgage Broker: A mortgage broker plays a crucial role as a specialized intermediary between investors and lenders, facilitating the financing process for the acquisition of income-generating properties. These professionals are highly knowledgeable about various loan products, lender requirements, and market conditions, enabling them to match investors with the most suitable mortgage options tailored to their investment objectives and financial circumstances. Mortgage brokers provide invaluable assistance throughout the financing process, guiding investors through the complex array of mortgage products, terms, and documentation requirements. They leverage their relationships with a network of lenders to negotiate competitive loan terms, including interest rates, loan amounts, and repayment schedules, on behalf of their clients. Additionally, mortgage brokers assist investors in preparing loan applications, gathering necessary financial documents, and navigating the underwriting process to secure mortgage approval efficiently. By leveraging the expertise and connections of a mortgage broker, investors can streamline the financing process, optimize loan terms, and ultimately enhance the profitability of their investment real estate endeavors.

Multiple Listing Service (MLS): The MLS is a comprehensive database used by real estate professionals to share information about properties for sale or rent. It serves as a centralized platform where real estate agents and brokers can access detailed listings of available properties, including information such as property features, photos, pricing, and contact details for the listing agent. The MLS enables agents to efficiently search and identify properties that meet their clients' specific criteria, streamlining the process of matching buyers or tenants with suitable properties. Additionally, the MLS facilitates cooperation and collaboration among real estate professionals by allowing them to share listings, market data, and commission arrangements. By listing properties on the MLS, sellers gain exposure to a wider audience of potential buyers or tenants, increasing the likelihood of a successful sale or lease. The MLS plays a crucial role in the real estate industry by providing a standardized platform for disseminating property information and facilitating transactions, ultimately benefiting both buyers and sellers.

Mutation: In real estate investing, mutation refers to the legal process of transferring property ownership from one person to another, typically recorded in government land records. This process is crucial for investors as it ensures that the new owner's name is officially updated in municipal or revenue records, thereby establishing clear and uncontested ownership. Mutation is essential not only for maintaining accurate property records but also for enabling the new owner to pay property taxes under their name and access utilities and municipal services. The process usually involves submitting an application to the local land revenue office along with necessary documents such as the sale deed, tax receipts, and a no-objection certificate (NOC) from the relevant authority. Timely and accurate mutation helps prevent legal disputes over property ownership and ensures smooth future transactions, including selling, mortgaging, or leasing the property. For investors, understanding and efficiently managing the mutation process is critical to securing their investment, establishing legal ownership, and avoiding potential legal complications that could affect property profitability and marketability.

N

National Association of Realtors (NAR): A comprehensive resource and advocate for real estate professionals and investors, the NAR provides a wealth of information, tools, and services that help investors make informed decisions in the rental property market. Membership offers access to extensive market data, research reports, and trend analyses that are crucial for understanding local and national real estate dynamics. NAR also offers educational programs and certifications, such as the Certified Residential Specialist (CRS) and Accredited Buyer's Representative (ABR), which equip investors with specialized knowledge and skills in property management, tenant relations, and investment strategies. Furthermore, NAR's advocacy efforts at the federal, state, and local levels ensure that the interests of real estate investors are represented in legislative and regulatory matters, helping to shape a favorable business environment. Through its Code of Ethics, NAR promotes high standards of professionalism and ethical conduct among its members, fostering trust and reliability in real estate transactions. Overall, the NAR is an indispensable ally for rental property investors, providing essential support, resources, and advocacy to enhance their investment success.

Negative Amortization: A situation where the principal balance of a loan increases over time rather than decreasing as it typically does with traditional amortizing loans. This occurs when the borrower's monthly payments are insufficient to cover the full amount of interest owed on the loan. As a result, the unpaid interest is added to the loan balance, causing it to grow instead of decrease. Negative amortization commonly occurs with certain types of ARMs, particularly those with introductory periods where the interest rate is fixed at a low initial rate. During this period, borrowers may make payments that do not fully cover the accruing interest, leading to negative amortization. While negative amortization can provide short-term affordability benefits by reducing initial payment obligations, it poses long-term risks for borrowers. As the loan balance grows, borrowers may face larger monthly payments or significant repayment challenges when the loan resets to a fully amortizing schedule. Additionally, negative amortization can erode equity in the property and increase the overall cost of borrowing over time. It's essential for borrowers to fully understand the implications of negative amortization and carefully consider its potential risks before selecting a mortgage product.

Net Operating Income (NOI): NOI is a crucial financial metric in rental property investment that reflects the property's profitability and cash flow potential. It represents the income generated from the property minus operating expenses, excluding debt service and income taxes. NOI is calculated by subtracting total operating expenses from the property's gross rental income. Operating expenses typically include property management fees, maintenance and repairs, property taxes, insurance, utilities, and any other expenses directly related to the operation and maintenance of the property. NOI provides investors with a clear picture of the property's income-producing ability, independent of financing and tax considerations. It serves as a key indicator of the property's financial health and investment performance, helping investors assess its viability and compare different investment opportunities. A positive NOI indicates that the property generates sufficient income to cover its operating expenses and provides a ROI, while a negative NOI suggests that the property is not generating enough income to cover its expenses. By analyzing NOI, investors can make informed decisions about property acquisitions, financing strategies, and overall portfolio management to maximize profitability and achieve their investment objectives in rental property ventures.

Non-Conforming Loan: A non-conforming loan, also known as a jumbo loan, represents a financing option that exceeds the loan limits set by government-sponsored entities such as Fannie Mae and Freddie Mac. These loans are often sought after for high-value properties that surpass the conventional loan limits, allowing investors to finance larger acquisitions without resorting to multiple mortgages or significant down payments. Non-conforming loans typically carry higher interest rates and stricter qualification requirements compared to conforming loans, as they pose greater risk to lenders due to their larger loan amounts and non-standard underwriting criteria. Investors opting for non-conforming loans may need to demonstrate strong creditworthiness, sufficient income, and substantial reserves to qualify. However, despite the stringent requirements, non-conforming loans offer flexibility and convenience for investors seeking to acquire high-end rental properties or multi-unit complexes. By providing access to larger loan amounts, non-conforming loans empower investors to diversify their portfolios, capitalize on lucrative investment opportunities, and maximize returns in the competitive rental property market.

NNN (Triple Net): A NNN (Triple Net) property is a type of commercial real estate arrangement where the tenant is responsible for paying not only the base rent but also the property taxes, insurance, and maintenance costs associated with the property. In essence, the tenant bears the majority of the operating expenses typically incurred by the property owner in addition to the rent. This arrangement shifts a significant portion of the financial and operational responsibilities from the landlord to the tenant, offering potential benefits such as predictable cash flow and reduced management oversight for the property owner. From the perspective of investors, NNN properties are often considered attractive due to their potential for stable and passive income streams, especially when leased to financially stable tenants with long-term leases. However, thorough due diligence is crucial to assess factors such as the creditworthiness of the tenant, the condition of the property, and the terms of the lease agreement. Additionally, investors should consider market conditions, location, and potential risks associated with the property before making an investment decision. Overall, NNN rental investment properties can be an appealing option for investors seeking low-maintenance, income-generating assets in the commercial real estate market.

O

Occupancy Certificate (OC): A crucial document in rental property investing, signifying that a property is fit for occupancy and complies with all relevant building codes and regulations. Issued by the local municipal authority or building department, the OC certifies that the construction of the building has been completed according to the approved plans and specifications, including adherence to safety norms, fire regulations, and structural standards. For investors, obtaining an OC is vital as it legally permits the property to be occupied, rented out, or sold. Without this certificate, the property might be deemed illegal, potentially leading to fines, legal complications, and difficulties in securing financing or insurance. Moreover, tenants often require an OC as a safeguard to ensure the property they are renting meets safety and regulatory standards. Therefore, ensuring that the property has a valid OC is essential for maintaining its marketability, attracting tenants, and protecting the investment from legal and financial risks. Understanding the process of obtaining an OC, which involves inspections and approval from various municipal departments, is fundamental for any real estate investor looking to ensure compliance and maximize the property's potential.

Offer: An offer represents a formal proposal made by a prospective buyer to purchase a property. It signifies a significant milestone in the home buying process and typically includes essential details such as the offered purchase price, proposed terms and conditions, and any contingencies or conditions that must be met for the offer to be considered valid. The offer may also specify other important aspects such as the desired closing date, financing arrangements, and included or excluded items in the sale. Once presented to the seller or their representative, the offer initiates a negotiation phase where the terms may be adjusted or countered before reaching a mutual agreement. Crafting a compelling offer requires careful consideration of market conditions, property value, and the buyer's financial situation. It's essential for buyers to work closely with their real estate agent to formulate a competitive offer that aligns with their budget and priorities while also appealing to the seller's preferences. Ultimately, a well-crafted offer is the first step toward securing a successful real estate transaction and acquiring the desired property.

Open House: An open house is an event organized by a seller or their real estate agent to showcase a property to potential buyers in a structured and open environment. Typically held during designated hours on a specific day, an open house invites interested buyers, agents, and sometimes even curious neighbors to explore the property firsthand. Open houses offer a unique opportunity for buyers to view the property in person, assess its layout, features, and overall condition, and envision themselves living in the space. For sellers, open houses provide a platform to attract a wide range of potential buyers and generate interest in the property. During an open house, visitors are free to tour the property at their leisure, ask questions, and gather information from the hosting agent.

Real estate agents often use open houses as a marketing tool to showcase the property's highlights, highlight its unique selling points, and create a sense of urgency among buyers. Additionally, open houses can facilitate face-to-face interactions between agents and potential buyers, fostering relationships and potentially leading to offers. Overall, open houses serve as a valuable component of the marketing strategy for selling a property, helping to maximize exposure and ultimately secure a successful sale.

Option Agreement: An option agreement is a legally binding contract between a property owner (the grantor) and a potential buyer or investor (the optionee) that grants the optionee the exclusive right to purchase the property within a specified period at an agreed-upon price. This contract typically involves the payment of an option fee by the optionee to the grantor, which grants the optionee the right to purchase the property at a later date. Option agreements provide flexibility and control to the optionee, allowing them to secure the property without the obligation to purchase it immediately. During the option period, the optionee may conduct due diligence, secure financing, and assess the property's potential before making a final decision to exercise the option. If the optionee chooses to proceed with the purchase, the option fee is typically applied toward the purchase price, while if they decide not to exercise the option, the option fee is usually forfeited to the grantor. Option agreements are commonly used in real estate transactions involving unique or high-value properties, as well as in situations where buyers require additional time to secure financing or complete feasibility studies. Overall, option agreements provide a valuable mechanism for both buyers and sellers to negotiate terms and secure agreements while mitigating risks and uncertainties associated with the purchase process.

P

Passive Income: In rental property investing, passive income refers to the earnings generated from rental properties with minimal active involvement from the investor. This type of income is highly appealing because it provides a steady revenue stream while allowing the investor to pursue other ventures or maintain a separate career. To achieve truly passive income, investors often rely on property management companies to handle day-to-day operations such as tenant screening, rent collection, maintenance, and repairs. The primary responsibilities of the investor are usually limited to initial property acquisition, securing financing, and periodic oversight to ensure the investment remains profitable. Rental income, when well-managed, can provide significant returns that appreciate over time due to property value increases and inflation-driven rent hikes. Additionally, rental properties offer tax advantages such as deductions for mortgage interest, property taxes, and depreciation. However, to maintain passive income, investors must conduct thorough due diligence before purchasing properties to ensure they are located in desirable areas with high rental demand, low vacancy rates, and strong potential for long-term appreciation. By carefully selecting and managing properties, investors can create a sustainable source of passive income that contributes to financial independence and long-term wealth building.

Portfolio Loan: A portfolio loan refers to a mortgage loan that is originated and held by the lender in their own investment portfolio, rather than being sold on the secondary mortgage market. Unlike conventional loans, which are often sold to GSEs like Fannie Mae or Freddie Mac, portfolio loans are kept by the originating lender, allowing them to set their own underwriting criteria and terms. Portfolio loans are commonly used for financing investment properties, including rental homes, multi-family buildings, or commercial real estate. Portfolio lenders may be more willing to finance investment properties than conventional lenders, however, since they retain the loans on their books, they assume the risk associated with the loans, including credit risk and interest rate risk. As a result, portfolio lenders may have stricter underwriting standards or charge higher interest rates to compensate for the increased risk.

Pre-approval: A pre-approval is a crucial step in the process of purchasing a property. It involves obtaining a commitment from a lender for a specific loan amount based on a thorough assessment of the borrower's financial information. Unlike pre-qualification, which provides an estimate of how much a borrower may be able to borrow based on self-reported financial information, pre-approval involves a comprehensive review of the borrower's credit history, income, assets, and DTI ratio. To obtain pre-approval, borrowers typically submit documentation such as pay stubs, tax returns, bank statements, and employment verification to the lender. Once verified, the lender assesses the borrower's financial profile and issues a pre-approval letter, indicating the maximum loan amount for which they qualify. Pre-approval demonstrates to sellers that the buyer is serious and financially capable of securing financing, enhancing their credibility and competitiveness in a competitive real estate market. Additionally, pre-approval enables buyers to narrow down their home search to properties within their budget and move forward with confidence when making offers. By obtaining pre-approval, buyers streamline the home buying process, gain a clear understanding of their purchasing power, and position themselves for success in securing their desired property.

Prepayment Penalty: A prepayment penalty is a fee charged by lenders if a borrower pays off a mortgage loan before its scheduled term ends. This penalty is typically outlined in the loan agreement and serves as a way for lenders to recoup a portion of the interest income they would have earned had the loan been paid according to the original terms. Prepayment penalties can take various forms, including a percentage of the outstanding loan balance or a certain number of months' worth of interest payments. While prepayment penalties are less common today, they were more prevalent in the past, particularly with subprime or ARM loans. These penalties can pose a significant financial burden for borrowers seeking to refinance their mortgage, sell their property, or make large lump-sum payments toward their loan principal. Therefore, it's crucial for borrowers to carefully review their loan documents and understand any prepayment penalty provisions before committing to a mortgage loan. In some cases, borrowers may negotiate with lenders to waive or reduce prepayment penalties as part of their loan agreement, especially if they anticipate paying off the loan early.

Pre-qualification Letter: A pre-qualification letter is a preliminary assessment provided by a lender to a prospective homebuyer based on self-reported financial information. This letter indicates the estimated loan amount that the buyer may qualify for based on their stated income, assets, debts, and credit score. Unlike pre-approval, which involves a more rigorous verification process and provides a firm commitment from the lender, pre-qualification is an informal evaluation that serves as a starting point for buyers to understand their potential borrowing capacity. While a pre-qualification letter does not guarantee financing or signify a formal commitment from the lender, it provides buyers with valuable information to guide their home search and offer decisions. Sellers may also request a pre-qualification letter from prospective buyers to assess their financial readiness and seriousness about purchasing a property. Although pre-qualification is a helpful initial step in the home buying process, buyers should ultimately seek pre-approval to obtain a more accurate assessment of their loan eligibility and strengthen their position when making offers on properties.

Principal: The original amount of money borrowed from a lender to finance the purchase of a property. It represents the initial debt owed by the investor to the lender, excluding interest and other fees. Repayment of the principal is a central aspect of mortgage financing, with investors making regular payments over the loan term to gradually reduce the outstanding balance. Each mortgage payment is typically divided between principal and interest, with a greater portion allocated to interest at the beginning of the loan term and gradually shifting toward principal over time. As investors pay down the principal, their equity in the property increases, and they gradually gain ownership of the asset outright. Additionally, reducing the principal balance through mortgage payments can improve the property's overall financial position and increase its potential profitability by lowering future interest expenses. Therefore, understanding and effectively managing the principal portion of a mortgage loan is essential for rental property investors to build equity, optimize cash flow, and achieve long-term financial success in the real estate market.

Principal, Interest, Taxes, and Insurance (PITI): PITI, an acronym for Principal, Interest, Taxes, and Insurance, represents the four primary components of a mortgage payment in real estate. Each element plays a crucial role in determining the total cost of homeownership and ensuring financial stability for both borrowers and lenders. The principal portion of the payment goes toward reducing the outstanding balance of the loan, while the interest represents the cost of borrowing money from the lender. Property taxes, assessed by local governments based on the property's assessed value, contribute to funding local services and infrastructure. Additionally, homeowners are required to maintain insurance coverage, including hazard insurance and, in some cases, mortgage insurance, to protect against potential damages or losses. Lenders often require borrowers to make monthly payments into an escrow account, from which property taxes and insurance premiums are paid on their behalf. The PITI payment provides a comprehensive overview of the total financial obligation associated with homeownership, allowing borrowers to budget effectively and plan for their housing expenses. By understanding and managing PITI payments, homeowners can ensure financial stability and mitigate risks associated with homeownership, such as potential property tax increases or insurance claims.

Private Mortgage Insurance (PMI): PMI is a safeguard for mortgage lenders in the real estate industry, particularly when borrowers are unable to make a down payment of 20% or more on their home purchase. Essentially, PMI serves as a protective measure, shielding lenders from potential financial loss if borrowers default on their mortgage payments. It allows individuals who may not have substantial savings for a large down payment to still qualify for a mortgage and purchase a home. PMI is typically a requirement for conventional loans with a down payment of less than 20% of the home's purchase price. Borrowers pay a monthly premium for PMI, which is added to their mortgage payment, increasing their overall cost of homeownership. However, as borrowers pay down their mortgage and build equity in the property, they can request the removal of PMI once they reach a certain LTV ratio, typically when their equity reaches 20%. Alternatively, PMI is automatically terminated when the loan balance reaches 78% of the original home value. While PMI increases the initial cost of homeownership, it plays a crucial role in making mortgages accessible to a broader range of buyers by reducing the barrier of a large down payment.

Property Appreciation: A fundamental aspect of rental property investing, embodying the potential for long-term wealth accumulation. This concept refers to the increase in the value of a property over time due to various factors such as market demand, economic growth, and improvements to the property itself. In rental property investing, appreciation plays a crucial role as it directly impacts the ROI for the property owner. As the property appreciates in value, its market worth increases, allowing investors to build equity and potentially sell the property for a profit in the future. Additionally, property appreciation can provide opportunities for leveraging equity to acquire additional properties or secure financing for other investments. However, it is important for investors to conduct thorough market research and due diligence to identify properties in areas with strong potential for appreciation, considering factors such as population growth, job market stability, and infrastructure development. While property appreciation can significantly enhance the overall profitability of rental property investments, it is essential for investors to adopt a long-term perspective and diversify their investment portfolio to mitigate risks associated with market fluctuations.

Property Insurance: Property insurance, also known as landlord insurance or rental property insurance, is a crucial component for anyone who owns residential or commercial properties and leases them out to tenants. This specialized insurance provides protection against a range of risks that landlords may face, offering financial security and peace of mind. Rental property insurance typically covers the physical structure of the building, including damage from events such as fire, storms, vandalism, and certain natural disasters. Additionally, it often includes liability coverage, which protects landlords from legal expenses and damages if a tenant or visitor is injured on the property and sues for negligence. Moreover, rental property insurance may offer coverage for loss of rental income in case the property becomes uninhabitable due to a covered event, helping landlords maintain their cash flow during repairs. It's important for landlords to carefully review their insurance policies to ensure they have adequate coverage tailored to their specific needs and the risks associated with their rental properties. By investing in rental property insurance, landlords can mitigate financial risks and safeguard their investments against unforeseen circumstances, allowing them to focus on maximizing their rental income and providing a safe and secure living environment for their tenants.

Property Management: The process of overseeing the day-to-day operations and maintenance of investment properties on behalf of the property owner. It involves a range of responsibilities, including tenant acquisition and retention, rent collection, property maintenance and repairs, lease enforcement, financial management, and compliance with legal regulations. Effective property management is essential for rental property investors to maximize the property's income potential, maintain its value, and ensure a positive experience for tenants. Professional property management companies or individual property managers are often hired to handle these tasks, particularly for investors who own multiple properties or lack the time or expertise to manage them personally. A competent property management team can help investors minimize vacancies, address tenant concerns promptly, enforce lease agreements, coordinate maintenance and repairs efficiently, and navigate legal and regulatory requirements effectively. Ultimately, outsourcing property management allows investors to focus on other aspects of their investment strategy while ensuring that their rental properties are well-maintained and profitable over the long term.

Property Tax: The tax levied by local governments on real estate properties owned by investors. It is a significant expense that investors must account for when evaluating the financial performance and profitability of rental properties. Property taxes are typically based on the assessed value of the property, determined by government assessors, and are used to fund various public services and infrastructure projects, such as schools, roads, and emergency services. The amount of property tax owed can vary depending on factors such as the property's location, size, and assessed value, as well as local tax rates and regulations. Property taxes are a recurring expense that investors must budget for and pay annually, often in multiple installments throughout the year. Prudent investors consider property taxes when assessing the overall operating expenses of a rental property and strive to manage them effectively to maximize cash flow and profitability. Strategies for managing property taxes may include appealing assessments, taking advantage of available tax exemptions or deductions, and staying informed about changes in local tax policies and regulations. Overall, understanding and managing property taxes are essential for rental property investors to optimize financial performance and achieve long-term success in the real estate market.

Purchase and Sale Agreement (P&S): A Purchase and Sale Agreement, also known as a Sales Contract or Purchase Agreement, is a legally binding contract between a buyer and a seller outlining the terms and conditions of a real estate transaction. This document serves as a roadmap for the sale of a property and typically includes the identification of Parties, Property Description, Purchase Price, Contingencies, Financing Details, Closing Date, Closing Costs, Property Condition, Seller's Obligations, Buyer's Obligations, Earnest Money Deposit, etc. Once both parties have agreed to the terms outlined in the

Purchase and Sale Agreement, and the document has been signed by both the buyer and seller, it becomes a legally binding contract. Failure to adhere to the terms of the agreement can result in legal consequences for the party in breach of the contract.

Q

Qualifying Ratios: Qualifying ratios play a pivotal role in rental property investment by assessing the financial stability and creditworthiness of potential borrowers seeking financing. These ratios, often used by lenders during the mortgage approval process, compare the borrower's income and debt obligations to determine their ability to manage additional debt associated with the rental property investment. The two primary qualifying ratios used in rental property investment are the DTI ratio and the LTV ratio. The DTI ratio compares the borrower's monthly debt payments to their gross monthly income, reflecting their capacity to take on additional debt. Lenders typically prefer borrowers with DTI ratios below a certain threshold to ensure they can comfortably afford their mortgage payments. The LTV ratio, on the other hand, compares the loan amount to the appraised value of the property, representing the borrower's equity stake and the lender's risk exposure. Lenders often impose maximum LTV ratios to mitigate risk and ensure adequate collateral coverage. By evaluating these qualifying ratios, lenders assess the borrower's financial health and determine their eligibility for financing, interest rates, and loan terms. For investors, understanding and managing qualifying ratios are crucial steps in securing financing for rental property investments and optimizing their overall financial strategy.

Quitclaim Deed: A legal document used to transfer ownership or interest in a property from one party to another without any warranties or guarantees regarding the property's title. Unlike a warranty deed, which provides assurances to the buyer regarding the seller's ownership and any potential encumbrances on the property, a quitclaim deed transfers whatever interest the grantor (seller) has in the property to the grantee (buyer) without making any promises about the title's validity or encumbrances. Quitclaim deeds are often used in situations where the transfer of ownership is between family members, in divorce proceedings, or to clear up title issues. While quitclaim deeds are relatively straightforward and expedient, they do not offer the same level of protection as warranty deeds, and buyers should conduct thorough due diligence to ensure the property's title is clear before accepting a quitclaim deed. Additionally, it's essential for both parties to fully understand the implications of using a quitclaim deed and seek legal advice if necessary to ensure their interests are protected in the property transfer process.

Quiet Title Action: A legal proceeding initiated to resolve disputes or uncertainties regarding the ownership or title of a property. This legal action seeks to "quiet" any conflicting claims or clouds on the title, thereby establishing a clear and marketable title for the property. Quiet title actions are typically filed by property owners or prospective buyers who encounter challenges or uncertainties regarding the ownership status of a property, such as conflicting property boundaries, undisclosed liens, or unresolved inheritance issues. Through the quiet title action process, the court reviews the evidence presented by all parties involved, including title documents, surveys, and witness testimony, to determine the rightful owner of the property and clarify any ambiguities in the title. Once the court issues a judgment in favor of the plaintiff, the title is effectively cleared of any competing claims or defects, providing assurance to the property owner or buyer and facilitating future real estate transactions. Quiet title actions are complex legal proceedings that require careful preparation and representation by experienced real estate attorneys to ensure a successful outcome and protect the interests of all parties involved. Real Estate Agent: A licensed professional who represents buyers or sellers in real estate transactions in exchange for a commission.

R

Real Estate Financial Modeling (REFM): A specialized analytical tool used to assess and predict the financial performance of investment properties. REFM involves creating intricate financial models that incorporate various revenue streams, such as rental income and ancillary income, and accounting for all potential expenses, including property management fees, maintenance costs, insurance, and property taxes. These models also integrate financing structures, including mortgage terms, interest rates, and loan amortization schedules. Key financial metrics, such as NOI, Cash Flow After Debt Service (CFADS), Internal Rate of Return (IRR), ROI, and DSCR, are calculated to evaluate the investment's viability and profitability. Sensitivity analysis within REFM allows investors to test different scenarios, such as changes in vacancy rates, rent growth, and operating expenses, to understand their impact on the investment's performance. By providing a comprehensive and dynamic financial overview, REFM helps investors make informed decisions, optimize property performance, and strategically plan for long-term investment success.

Real Estate Investment Trust (REIT): A REIT is a company that owns, operates, or finances income-generating real estate. REITs pool the capital of numerous investors to purchase a portfolio of properties, which can include office buildings, apartments, hotels, shopping centers, and more. One of the key features of REITs is that they must distribute at least 90% of their taxable income to shareholders in the form of dividends. This characteristic makes them attractive to income-seeking investors. Additionally, REITs often provide diversification benefits to investors who want exposure to real estate without directly owning physical properties. REITs can be publicly traded on major stock exchanges like any other publicly traded company, or they can be privately held. They offer investors an opportunity to invest in real estate without the hassle of directly buying, managing, or financing properties.

Real Estate Owned (REO): A term used in the real estate industry to describe properties that have been foreclosed upon and are now owned by a lender or financial institution. These properties were previously mortgaged by homeowners who defaulted on their loan payments, leading to foreclosure proceedings initiated by the lender. After the foreclosure process is completed and the property fails to sell at auction, it becomes REO by the lender. REO properties are typically sold by the lender through a real estate agent or broker, often at a discounted price compared to market value, in an effort to recoup as much of the outstanding loan balance as possible. These properties may vary in condition, ranging from well-maintained to requiring significant repairs or renovations. Investors and homebuyers often view REO properties as potential investment opportunities, as they may offer the chance to purchase real estate below market value. However, purchasing an REO property can come with its own set of challenges, including potential liens, title issues, and competition from other buyers. Overall, REO properties represent a segment of the real estate market that requires specialized knowledge and expertise to navigate effectively.

Referral Fee: A compensation paid to an individual or entity for referring a client or customer to a real estate agent or brokerage. This fee is typically a percentage of the commission earned by the agent upon the successful completion of a transaction initiated by the referral. Referral fees are common within the industry and serve as a way to incentivize individuals, such as other agents, past clients, or even professionals in related fields like mortgage brokers or attorneys, to recommend the services of a particular real estate agent or brokerage. These fees can vary depending on local regulations, market practices, and the specifics of the referral arrangement. While referral fees can be beneficial for expanding one's network and generating leads, it's crucial for all parties involved to adhere to legal and ethical guidelines to ensure transparency and fair practices in real estate transactions. Additionally, disclosure of referral fees is often required to maintain transparency and compliance with regulations governing the real estate industry.

Refinance: The process of replacing an existing mortgage with a new loan, typically to take advantage of better terms, lower interest rates, or access equity in the property. Homeowners may choose to refinance their mortgage for various reasons, including reducing monthly payments, shortening the loan term, consolidating debt, or funding home improvements. Refinancing can offer financial benefits by lowering the interest rate, which can result in substantial savings over the life of the loan. Additionally, refinancing to a shorter loan term can help homeowners build equity faster and pay off their mortgage sooner. Cash-out refinancing allows homeowners to access the equity they've built up in their property by borrowing more than the remaining balance on their mortgage and receiving the difference in cash. While refinancing can offer significant financial advantages, it's essential for homeowners to carefully consider the costs and implications of refinancing, including closing costs, loan fees, and potential changes to loan terms. Working with a knowledgeable mortgage lender or financial advisor can help homeowners evaluate their options and determine if refinancing is the right decision for their financial goals and circumstances.

Rental Agent: A rental agent, also known as a leasing agent or rental broker, is a professional within the real estate industry who specializes in assisting individuals or businesses with finding and leasing rental properties. Their primary role is to act as intermediaries between landlords and tenants, helping both parties navigate the rental process efficiently and effectively. Rental agents possess in-depth knowledge of the local rental market, including current rental rates, available properties, and neighborhood amenities, allowing them to match tenants with suitable rental options based on their preferences and budget. They provide valuable guidance and assistance to tenants throughout the rental search process, from identifying potential properties and scheduling viewings to negotiating lease terms and completing rental applications. Additionally, rental agents often handle administrative tasks such as preparing lease agreements, conducting background and credit checks on prospective tenants, and coordinating move-in logistics. Their expertise and professionalism streamline the rental process for both landlords and tenants, ensuring a smooth and successful rental experience.

Rental Yield: A crucial metric used to evaluate the financial performance and profitability of an investment property. It represents the annual income generated from renting out a property relative to its value or purchase price. Rental yield is typically expressed as a percentage and can be calculated in two primary ways: gross rental yield and net rental yield. Gross rental yield is calculated by dividing the property's annual rental income by its purchase price or market value, excluding any expenses. Net rental yield, on the other hand, factors in operating expenses such as property taxes, insurance, maintenance, vacancies, and property management fees, providing a more accurate reflection of the property's profitability. A higher rental yield indicates a more lucrative investment opportunity, as it signifies greater potential income relative to the property's value. However, it's essential for investors to consider other factors such as location, market trends, tenant demand, and potential for capital appreciation when assessing rental yield. While high rental yield properties may offer attractive cash flow potential, they may also come with higher risks or lower long-term growth prospects. Therefore, savvy investors carefully analyze rental yield alongside other key metrics to make informed investment decisions and optimize their rental property portfolios for long-term success.

Return on Investment (ROI): A crucial metric that gauges the profitability and efficiency of an investment in real estate. It is calculated by dividing the net profit from the rental property by the total investment cost, then multiplying by 100 to express it as a percentage. For rental properties, net profit typically includes rental income minus operating expenses such as property management fees, maintenance costs, property taxes, insurance, and any mortgage payments. A high ROI indicates that the property is generating substantial earnings relative to the invested capital, making it an attractive investment. Factors influencing ROI in rental properties include location, property condition, rental demand, and market trends. Investors often seek properties in high-demand areas with the potential for appreciation to maximize ROI. Additionally, managing expenses effectively and maintaining high occupancy rates are essential strategies to enhance ROI. Understanding and calculating ROI provides investors with a clear picture of financial performance and helps in making informed decisions about acquiring, holding, or selling rental properties.

S

Seller's Agent: A seller's agent, also known as a listing agent, is a licensed real estate professional who represents the interests of the property seller in a real estate transaction. Their primary responsibility is to assist the seller in marketing and selling their property for the best possible price and terms. Listing agents typically provide a range of services, including conducting market research to determine the property's value, advising the seller on preparing the property for sale, creating and implementing a marketing plan to attract potential buyers, coordinating property showings and open houses, negotiating offers on behalf of the seller, and guiding the seller through the closing process. Additionally, listing agents serve as intermediaries between the seller and prospective buyers, facilitating communication and addressing any concerns or questions that may arise during the sales process. Their expertise in pricing strategies, market trends, and negotiation skills are invaluable assets to sellers, helping them achieve their goals and maximize their returns on the sale of their property. Short Sale: A sale of real estate in which the proceeds fall short of the balance owed on the property's mortgage, requiring approval from the lender.

Survey: A detailed examination or assessment of a property's boundaries, features, and potential encumbrances conducted by a licensed surveyor. The survey provides critical information about the property's physical characteristics, including its dimensions, boundary lines, easements, and any improvements such as buildings, fences, or utilities. Surveys are essential in real estate transactions as they help verify the property's legal description, identify any encroachments or boundary disputes, and ensure compliance with local zoning and land use regulations. Additionally, surveys play a crucial role in mitigating risks for buyers and lenders by providing clarity and certainty regarding the property's boundaries and potential limitations. Depending on the type of survey conducted, such as a boundary survey, ALTA/NSPS survey, or topographic survey, the surveyor may use various techniques and technologies, including GPS, GIS, and aerial photography, to accurately map and document the property. While surveys are not always required in real estate transactions, they are highly recommended to protect the interests of all parties involved and prevent potential legal disputes or issues in the future. Buyers and sellers should carefully review survey reports and address any concerns or discrepancies with the assistance of legal counsel or real estate professionals to ensure a smooth and successful transaction.

Syndicate: In real estate, a syndicate refers to a group of individuals or entities who come together to pool their financial resources and expertise to invest in a real estate project. These projects can vary widely in scope, from acquiring a single property to developing a large-scale commercial complex. A syndicate is formed by a lead investor or sponsor who identifies an investment opportunity. This sponsor then seeks out other investors who are interested in participating in the project. The syndicate members or investors contribute funds to the project based on their agreed-upon investment amounts. The sponsor typically manages the syndicate and makes decisions regarding the acquisition, management, and disposition of the real estate assets. Syndicate members typically own shares or interests in the real estate project proportionate to their investment contributions. The ownership structure can vary, with some members having more active roles in decision-making and management, while others may take a more passive investment approach. Profits generated from real estate investments, such as rental income or proceeds from property sales, are distributed among syndicate members according to their ownership stakes. These profits are typically distributed after expenses and any debt obligations associated with the project have been met. Real estate syndication allows individual investors to access larger and potentially more lucrative investment opportunities that they might not be able to pursue on their own. It also enables investors to diversify their portfolios by spreading their investments across multiple properties or projects. However, it's important for syndicate members to conduct thorough due diligence and carefully review the terms of the syndication agreement before committing their funds.

T

Tenancy-at-Will (TAW): A rental arrangement in real estate where a tenant occupies a property with the landlord's consent but without a formal lease agreement or set duration. This type of tenancy is typically more flexible than traditional leases, allowing the landlord or the tenant to terminate the arrangement at any time, usually with a notice period that varies by jurisdiction. This flexibility is advantageous for investors who want to sell or repurpose the property without the constraints of a long-term lease. However, it also introduces uncertainty, as the tenant may leave at short notice, potentially leading to periods of vacancy and loss of rental income. Additionally, laws governing tenancies at will can differ significantly by location, affecting both the landlord's and tenant's rights and obligations. Property investors must understand these nuances and incorporate them into their investment strategies, balancing the potential benefits of flexibility with the risks of instability.

Title: A title refers to the legal right to ownership of a property, including all associated rights and interests. A clear and marketable title is essential for any real estate transaction, as it provides assurance to buyers and lenders that the seller has the legal authority to transfer ownership of the property. Title is typically conveyed through a deed, which is a legal document that transfers ownership from the seller (grantor) to the buyer (grantee). Before a property can be sold or transferred, a title search is conducted to examine public records and verify the chain of ownership, any existing liens, encumbrances, or restrictions, and ensure that the title is free from defects or clouds. Title insurance is also commonly obtained to protect buyers and lenders against any unforeseen issues or challenges that may arise with the title after the transaction is completed. A clear and marketable title is crucial for buyers to obtain financing, secure ownership rights, and protect their investment in the property. Therefore, it's essential for buyers to conduct due diligence and work with experienced real estate professionals to ensure that the title is properly researched and conveyed during the transaction process.

Title Insurance: Title insurance is a critical component of real estate transactions that protects buyers and lenders against financial loss due to title defects, liens, or other issues that may arise with a property's ownership rights. Unlike other forms of insurance that protect against future events, title insurance provides coverage for past events that may affect the property's title. During the closing process, a title search is conducted to examine public records and verify the property's ownership history, liens, encumbrances, and other potential title defects. However, even with a thorough title search, there may still be undiscovered issues or challenges that could jeopardize the buyer's ownership rights. Title insurance provides peace of mind by mitigating these risks and ensuring that buyers and lenders are protected against any unforeseen claims or challenges to the property's title. If a title defect or claim arises after the transaction is completed, the title insurance policy covers the costs associated with defending the title and resolving the issue, up to the policy's coverage limit. Title insurance is typically paid for by the buyer as a one-time premium at the time of closing and remains in effect for as long as the buyer or their heirs own the property. By providing financial protection and security, title insurance plays a crucial role in facilitating real estate transactions and protecting the interests of buyers and lenders in the property.

Transfer Tax: A tax imposed by state, county, or local governments on the transfer of real property from one owner to another. This tax is typically calculated as a percentage of the property's sale price or fair market value and is paid by the seller or buyer, depending on local regulations and customs. Transfer taxes are used by governments to generate revenue and fund various public services and initiatives, such as infrastructure projects, schools, and public safety programs. The amount of transfer tax owed varies widely depending on the location of the property and the applicable tax rates, which may be fixed or based on a sliding scale. In some cases, transfer tax exemptions or discounts may be available for certain types of transactions, such as transfers between family members or first-time homebuyers. It's essential for buyers and sellers to factor transfer taxes into their closing costs when budgeting for a real estate transaction and consult with a real estate attorney or tax professional to understand the specific tax implications in their area. By understanding and planning for transfer taxes, buyers and sellers can ensure a smooth and financially sound real estate transaction.

U

Underwriting: The process of evaluating the financial risk associated with extending a mortgage loan to a borrower. This comprehensive assessment involves reviewing the borrower's creditworthiness, financial history, and the property itself to determine the likelihood of repayment and the appropriate terms for the loan. Underwriting is typically conducted by a mortgage lender or financial institution and is guided by established lending criteria and risk assessment guidelines. The underwriting process begins with the submission of a loan application and supporting documentation by the borrower, including income verification, asset statements, credit reports, and property appraisals. The underwriter carefully reviews these documents to assess the borrower's ability to repay the loan, considering factors such as income stability, DTI ratio, credit score, and the property's value and condition. Based on this evaluation, the underwriter determines whether to approve, deny, or conditionally approve the loan, as well as the terms and conditions, including the loan amount, interest rate, and repayment schedule. Underwriting plays a crucial role in mitigating risks for lenders and ensuring responsible lending practices, while also providing borrowers with access to financing that meets their needs and financial circumstances. By conducting thorough underwriting, lenders can make informed decisions that balance the interests of both parties and promote the stability and sustainability of the real estate market.

Upfront Mortgage Insurance Premium (UFMIP): A fee paid by borrowers at the time of closing for certain types of mortgage loans, including FHA loans. This premium serves as an insurance policy that protects lenders against losses in the event of borrower default and foreclosure. The UFMIP is typically a one-time, upfront payment that is added to the borrower's loan amount and financed over the life of the loan. The amount of the UFMIP is calculated as a percentage of the loan amount and varies depending on the loan program and the borrower's creditworthiness. For FHA loans, the UFMIP rate is standardized and set by the FHA. The UFMIP payment helps fund the FHA's Mutual Mortgage Insurance (MMI) Fund, which covers losses incurred by lenders due to borrower defaults. While the UFMIP increases the upfront costs for borrowers, it allows them to qualify for mortgage loans with lower down payment requirements and more lenient credit criteria. By spreading the cost of mortgage insurance over the life of the loan, the UFMIP enables borrowers to achieve homeownership with more affordable financing options.

USDA Loan: A mortgage loan program offered by the United States Department of Agriculture (USDA) to encourage homeownership in rural and eligible suburban areas. Designed to assist low-to-moderate-income individuals and families, USDA loans offer favorable terms, including no down payment requirement and competitive interest rates. These loans are primarily targeted at buyers who may not qualify for traditional financing or struggle to afford a down payment on a home. To qualify for a USDA loan, the property must be located in a designated rural area as defined by the USDA, which typically includes towns with populations of fewer than 20,000 residents. Additionally, borrowers must meet income eligibility requirements based on the area's median income. USDA loans can be used to purchase existing homes or new construction or to finance repairs and improvements on eligible properties. The USDA loan program also offers options for refinancing existing mortgages to reduce monthly payments or access equity. Overall, USDA loans provide an accessible and affordable financing option for individuals and families seeking homeownership opportunities in rural and underserved areas, contributing to the stability and vitality of rural communities across the United States.

V

VA Loan: A mortgage loan guaranteed by the United States Department of Veterans Affairs, to specifically assist active-duty service members, veterans, and eligible surviving spouses in achieving homeownership. VA loans offer several advantages, including no down payment requirement, competitive interest rates, and the absence of PMI, making them an attractive option for eligible borrowers. These loans are issued by private lenders, such as banks and mortgage companies, and are backed by the VA, which assumes a portion of the loan's risk, thereby reducing the lender's exposure. VA loans can be used to purchase a primary residence, including single-family homes, condominiums, and multi-unit properties, or to refinance an existing mortgage. Additionally, VA loans offer flexible qualification requirements, including more lenient credit scores and DTI ratio guidelines, making homeownership more accessible to veterans and military personnel. The VA loan program also provides various protections for borrowers, such as limits on closing costs and fees, as well as assistance for borrowers facing financial hardship. Overall, VA loans play a crucial role in fulfilling the homeownership aspirations of military members and veterans, honoring their service and sacrifices while promoting stability and prosperity in their communities.

Variable-Rate Mortgage: A variable-rate mortgage, also known as an ARM, is a type of mortgage loan in which the interest rate fluctuates over time based on changes in a specified financial index. Unlike fixed-rate mortgages, where the interest rate remains constant for the entire term of the loan, the interest rate on a variable-rate mortgage is subject to periodic adjustments, typically at predetermined intervals such as annually or every few years. The initial interest rate on a variable-rate mortgage is often lower than that of a fixed-rate mortgage, making it an attractive option for borrowers seeking lower initial monthly payments or those who anticipate interest rates to decrease in the future. However, variable-rate mortgages come with inherent risks, as interest rates can rise over time, leading to higher monthly payments and increased borrowing costs for borrowers. To mitigate these risks, variable-rate mortgages often include rate adjustment caps, which limit the amount by which the interest rate can increase or decrease at each adjustment period, as well as lifetime caps, which impose a maximum limit on the total interest rate increase over the life of the loan. Borrowers considering a variable-rate mortgage should carefully evaluate their financial situation, consider potential future interest rate movements, and assess their ability to manage potential payment increases before selecting this type of loan.

Verification of Employment (VOE): A crucial step in the mortgage underwriting process that involves confirming the employment status and income of the borrower to assess their ability to repay the loan. Lenders typically request a VOE directly from the borrower's employer or through a third-party verification service. The VOE typically includes information such as the borrower's job title, employment start date, income verification, and the likelihood of continued employment. Lenders use the information provided in the VOE to verify the borrower's income stability, employment history, and capacity to manage mortgage payments. VOE is particularly important for self-employed borrowers or those with non-traditional employment arrangements, as it helps lenders assess their income consistency and financial reliability. Inaccurate or incomplete information in the VOE can delay the mortgage approval process or result in loan denial. Therefore, borrowers must ensure that the information provided in the VOE is accurate and up-to-date to facilitate a smooth mortgage application process and secure financing for their real estate purchase.

W

Walk-Through: The final inspection conducted by buyers shortly before the closing of a property sale. This critical step allows buyers to physically inspect the property to ensure it is in the same condition as when they agreed to purchase it and that any agreed-upon repairs or conditions have been satisfactorily completed. During the walk-through, buyers typically examine the interior and exterior of the property, checking for any visible damages, defects, or issues that may have arisen since their last visit. Common areas of focus include plumbing fixtures, electrical outlets, appliances, doors, windows, walls, and floors. Additionally, buyers may confirm that any items included in the sale, such as appliances or fixtures, are present and in working order. If the walk-through reveals any new issues or discrepancies, buyers can address them with the seller before the closing to ensure they are resolved to their satisfaction. The walk-through provides buyers with peace of mind and reassurance that the property meets their expectations before finalizing the transaction, thereby minimizing the risk of post-closing disputes or issues.

Warranty Deed: A legal document used to transfer ownership of a property from the seller (grantor) to the buyer (grantee), guaranteeing that the seller holds a clear and marketable title to the property and has the legal right to transfer ownership. This type of deed provides the highest level of protection for the buyer, as it includes specific warranties or promises made by the seller regarding the title and condition of the property. These warranties typically include assurances that the seller has the legal authority to sell the property, that the property is free from any undisclosed encumbrances or defects, and that the seller will defend the title against any future claims. By accepting a warranty deed, the buyer can be confident that they are receiving clear and unencumbered title to the property, backed by the seller's assurances and legal protections. If title issues or defects arise after the sale, the buyer may have legal recourse against the seller under the terms of the warranty deed. Warranty deeds are commonly used in residential real estate transactions to provide buyers with peace of mind and assurance that their ownership rights are protected.

Wholesaling: A real estate strategy where an investor, known as the wholesaler, identifies opportunities to purchase properties at a discounted price and then sells the rights to purchase that property to another buyer for a profit. In the context of rental properties, this strategy involves finding properties with the potential for generating rental income, negotiating a purchase agreement with the seller at a below-market price, and then assigning or selling that contract to a landlord or investor who intends to own and manage the property as a rental. Wholesaling in rental property investing can be an attractive option for investors looking to generate income without the long-term commitment and responsibilities of property ownership. Success in wholesaling requires a solid understanding of the local real estate market, the ability to identify properties with potential for rental income, and strong negotiation skills to secure favorable purchase agreements. Additionally, wholesalers must ensure compliance with real estate laws and regulations to conduct transactions ethically and legally.

Y

Yield: A critical metric that measures the annual income generated by an investment property as a percentage of its cost or current market value. This performance indicator helps investors gauge the profitability and efficiency of their investment. Yield is typically calculated using two main methods: gross yield and net yield. Gross yield is derived by dividing the annual rental income by the property's purchase price or current market value, providing a straightforward overview of income potential. However, net yield offers a more precise evaluation by factoring in additional expenses such as property management fees, maintenance costs, taxes, insurance, and vacancy rates. A higher yield indicates a more lucrative investment, making it an attractive option for investors seeking steady cash flow and long-term capital appreciation. Understanding and analyzing yield allows investors to compare different properties, assess market conditions, and make informed decisions that align with their financial goals. By carefully evaluating yield, investors can optimize their rental property portfolios to maximize returns and ensure sustainable growth.

Z

Zoning: A crucial consideration that directly impacts the potential use, development, and profitability of a property. Zoning regulations established by local governments dictate the allowable uses of land within specific areas, delineating zones for residential, commercial, industrial, or mixed-use purposes. Understanding zoning laws is essential for rental property investors as they determine what types of rental properties can be developed or operated in a particular location. For instance, residential zoning may restrict the construction of commercial properties or limit the number of units that can be built on a single lot. Investors must conduct thorough research on zoning ordinances and regulations before purchasing or developing rental properties to ensure compliance with local zoning laws. Failure to adhere to zoning requirements can result in fines, legal disputes, or even forced property closures, negatively impacting the investment's profitability and viability. Additionally, zoning regulations may influence rental property investment strategies, guiding investors to focus on areas where zoning permits high-density residential developments or mixed-use properties that cater to diverse tenant demographics and market demand. Overall, zoning regulations play a critical role in shaping the rental property investment landscape, influencing property values, rental income potential, and long-term investment outcomes.

1031 Exchange: A 1031 exchange, named after Section 1031 of the Internal Revenue Code of the IRS, is a powerful tool in rental property investing for deferring capital gains taxes. This provision allows investors to sell a rental property and reinvest the proceeds into a like-kind property, deferring the payment of capital gains taxes that would typically be due upon the sale. The primary benefit of a 1031 exchange is the ability to preserve the equity from the sale and reinvest it into another property without immediate tax consequences, thereby allowing investors to leverage their gains for further real estate acquisitions. This strategy is particularly advantageous for investors looking to diversify or upgrade their property portfolio without losing a significant portion of their profits to taxes. However, it is essential to comply with the strict rules and timelines set forth by the IRS for executing a 1031 exchange, including identifying potential replacement properties within 45 days of the initial sale and completing the acquisition within 180 days. Overall, utilizing a 1031 exchange can be a valuable tool for rental property investors seeking to optimize their tax liabilities and maximize their investment returns over the long term.

Printed in the USA
CPSIA information can be obtained
at www.ICGtesting.com
LVHW091938051124
795786LV00001B/1